THE 100 BEST
DIVIDEND-PAYING
STOCKS
TO OWN IN AMERICA

2005 Edition

Gene Walden

MARATHON
INTERNATIONAL BOOK CO.

MARATHON INTERNATIONAL BOOK COMPANY
P.O. Box 40 • Madison, IN 47250-0040 U.S.A.
Telephone (812) 273-4672 • Fax (812) 273-8964
E-mail: jwortham@seidata.com • Web site: www.marathonbooks.biz

Cover design: Otteau Christiansen

Library of Congress Cataloging-in-Publication Data

Walden, Gene.
  The 100 best dividend-paying stocks to own in America / Gene Walden.--
1st ed.
    p. cm.
  Includes index.
  ISBN 1-928877-05-2 (alk. paper)
  1. Stocks--United States. 2. Dividends--United States. 3. Investments--
United States. I. Title: One hundred best dividend-paying stocks to own in
America. II. Title.
  HG4963.W348 2005
  332.63'22--dc22

                                2004028401

First Edition • First Printing
Printed on acid-free paper
Printed and bound in the United States of America

This book is dedicated to the memory of Marcos Warner, my next door neighbor and the father of three boys (Luke, Jack and Harrison), whose upbeat spirit never wavered in his courageous battle with cancer.

It is also dedicated to Larry Nelson, my close friend and the research coordinator for most of my books over the past 15 years, who is facing a similar battle with that same sense of courage and high-spirited resolve.

Also by Gene Walden

The 100 Best Stocks to Own in America (7 editions)

The 100 Best Mutual Funds to Own in America (4 editions)

100 Ways to Beat the Market

If Not Stocks, What?

EDGAR: The Investor's Guide to Making Better Investments

The 100 Best Stocks for Under $25 (2 editions)

The 100 Best Technology Stocks (2 editions)

The Hot 100 Emerging Growth Stocks (2 editions)

Folio Phenomenon

The 100 Best Stocks to Own in the World

The H&R Block Just Smart Guide Personal Finance Advisor

Marketing Masters: Secrets of America's Best Companies

America's New Blue Chips

Winning with Your Stockbroker in Good Times and Bad

Table of Contents

Alphabetical List of
The 100 Best Dividend-Paying Stocks

Company (Ranking)

Abbott Laboratories (42)
ABM (71)
Air Products (95)
Alliance Capital Management (97)
Alltel (56)
Ameren (83)
AmSouth (22)
Archstone (20)
Associated Banc-Corp. (14)
Astoria (28)
Atmos (46)
Avery Dennison (70)
Bandag, Inc. (79)
Bank of America (3)
Bank of Nova Scotia (6)
BB&T (21)
BellSouth (81)
Black Hills Corp. (36)
Bristol-Myers Squibb (50)
Buckeye Partners (34)
California Water (86)
Canadian Imperial Bank (75)
Cedar Fair (13)
ChevronTexaco (73)
Cincinnati Financial (43)
Cinergy (85)
Coca-Cola (58)
Comerica (45)
ConAgra (29)
Consolidated Edison (62)
Dominion Resources (96)
Donnelley (R. R.) & Sons (78)
Duke Realty (17)
Emerson Electric (74)
Energy East (82)
Entergy (93)
Equity Residential Properties Trust (63)

ExxonMobile (94)
Fifth Third Bancorp (9)
First Horizon (11)
FPL Group (51)
General Electric (44)
Genuine Parts (53)
Great Plains Energy (84)
Health Care Property Investors (48)
Healthcare Realty Trust (59)
Jefferson-Pilot (26)
Johnson & Johnson (32)
Kimberly-Clark (72)
Kimco Realty (19)
Kinder Morgan Energy Partners (1)
Liberty Property Trust (33)
Lincoln National (52)
Mack-Cali Realty (60)
Marathon Oil (100)
May Department Stores (77)
MBNA Corp. (16)
Merck (57)
Mercury General (67)
National Bank of Canada (47)
National Fuel Gas (38)
New Plan Excel Realty Trust (90)
New Jersey Resources (66)
North Fork Bank (4)
NSTAR (49)
Peoples Bank (27)
Peoples Energy (24)
Piedmont Natural Gas (37)
Pinnacle West Capital (35)
Pitney Bowes (54)
PP&G (80)
Procter & Gamble (55)
Progress Energy (61)
Quaker Chemical (69)

Regions Financial (25)
Royal Bank of Canada (12)
RPM (68)
Sara Lee (30)
SBC (64)
ServiceMaster (76)
Spain Fund (99)
Stanley Works (88)
SunTrust Banks (15)
Synovus Financial (8)
TCF Financial (31)
Telefonos de Mexico (65)
Telecom Corp. of New Zealand (92)

Teppco Partners (18)
Thornburg Mortgage (2)
Total S.A. (10)
TransCanada Corp. (91)
Unitrin, Inc. (87)
U.S. Bancorp. (7)
Verizon (98)
V.F. Corp. (89)
Washington Federal (40)
Weingarten Realty Partners (23)
Wells Fargo (5)
Wilmington Trust. (41)
WPS Resources (39)

Acknowledgments

Without the contributions of several key individuals, this book would not have been possible. First I want to thank the person who gave me the idea for this book, my father, James Walden, who will celebrate his 90th birthday this year. As he put it, "you need to do a book on dividend-paying stocks because that's about the only investment left that pays a decent income." It was hard to argue with that logic. Fortunately, my publisher, Jim Wortham, agreed, and was happy to add this book to his growing list of investment titles. He has been very involved in helping me develop the concept and the content of the book. I also want to thank Sue Fossett, who did a terrific job of editing and laying out the copy in this book. And finally, I want to thank Otteau Christiansen, who understands that people *do* judge a book by its cover. He did a spectacular job of designing and producing the jacket for this book.

– GW

Introduction: The New Game in Town

THERE'S A NEW GAME IN TOWN FOR INCOME-ORIENTED INVESTORS—THANKS to some new tax legislation that makes stock dividends more attractive than ever.

While stock dividends have always had a certain allure for income investors, the new law makes dividends an income source that's almost too good to be true. Consider:

Tax advantages. The new law limits federal income tax on dividends to a maximum of 15 percent, even for those in the highest tax bracket. If you're in a lower bracket, you could pay as little as 5 percent (or less) on stock dividends. That gives dividends a big advantage over certificates of deposit, corporate bonds, mortgage-backed bonds, bank savings accounts, and even U.S. Treasury Bonds and Notes, all of which are fully taxable by the federal government. The only traditional income source that's better for taxes is municipal bonds, which are exempt from federal taxes, but typically pay a yield well below other types of bonds.

Solid returns. In the current low interest rate environment, many stocks pay dividends that are higher than most other income sources. On average, the 100 stocks featured in this book pay a dividend yield of about 4.1 percent—and many pay 5 to 8 percent—which is higher than most CDs, savings accounts, Treasury issues, municipal bonds, and investment grade corporate bonds.

Increasing stream of income. Stock dividends provide one advantage that you can't get with nearly any other type of income-oriented investment—an increasing stream of income. The vast majority of the stocks in this book have raised their dividend nearly every year for the past 10 years or more. Typically, those dividends have gone up 5 to 10 percent per year, and in many cases, they've climbed even faster. That's a huge benefit for investors who rely on investment income to pay their bills. Unlike standard fixed income investments, such as CDs and bonds, which pay a static rate through to maturity, rising stock dividends can help you maintain buying power by matching or exceeding the rate of inflation.

Not affected by market interest rate fluctuations. Most bonds are affected by interest rate fluctuations. When market interest rates rise, the value of existing bonds decline. Why? Example: if you bought a $1,000 bond a year ago that pays 4 percent, and now you can buy a $1,000 bond that pays 6 percent, no one would be willing to pay you the full $1,000 for a 4 percent bond. The current resale value of your bond would drop dramatically. That is not an issue with dividend-paying stocks.

Not callable. While bond values do indeed drop in a rising interest rate environment, they also tend to rise in a declining interest rate environment. However, many bonds are "callable," which means that when interest rates start dropping, corporations and municipalities often call in the bonds by refunding bondholders' money. Then they reissue new bonds at a lower interest rate. As a bondholder, you get your money back, but you no longer receive the higher interest return. That wouldn't happen with stock dividends.

Potential for capital appreciation. One other advantage of stocks is that, not only do they pay dividends, they also offer the potential for stock price appreciation. And, while stocks can be volatile and can drop in value, on average, stocks have gone up 10.7 percent per year over the past 100 years. So the odds are that you will not only receive a steady stream of dividend income, you will also see the value of your investment appreciate over time.

No question, dividend-paying stocks can also have some downside risks. They offer no guarantees, the stock can decline in value (in some cases dramatically), and the company may not always raise the dividend. In fact, dividends can be cut if times get tough. But as part of a diversified portfolio, a selection of solid dividend-paying stocks can provide a number of outstanding benefits for income-oriented investments. And the new tax law that gives dividends a big advantage over most fixed income investments is the icing on the cake.

Using this book

This book includes profiles on each of the *100 Best Dividend-Paying Stocks*. The profiles include:

The company's name address, phone number, stock symbol, web site address, and key officers

Current dividend yield (as of 2004). The dividend yield is similar to a rate of interest. It is the percentage of return the shareholder receives for each share of stock owned. It is calculated by dividing the annual dividend payout by the stock price. For instance, a $10 stock with a $1 annual dividend would have a 10 percent yield (1 divided by 10).

Back-to-the-Future Yield (see next section).

A ratings box that shows the stock's score by category and total score. (See more details in the upcoming section titled "Rating the Companies.")

A profile of several paragraphs summarizing the company's business operations

A section that explains the stock's point ratings for each of the four categories

A financial "Summary," that shows the company's dividend payment, earnings per share, revenue (or assets), and dividend yield for the past five years.

By reading through a company's profile, you should be able to get a quick read on its operations, its financial strength and its dividend yield and dividend growth.

The Back-to-the-Future Yield

The *Back-to-the-future yield* refers to the yield that a company's current dividend payout represents based on the purchase price of the stock in past years. For instance, if you had purchased a stock ten years ago for $10 a share, and that stock now pays an annual dividend of $1 per share, your 10-year *back-to-the future yield* would be 10 percent ($1 divided by $10). If you had purchased the same stock five years ago for $20 a share, your 5-year *back-to-the-future yield* would be 5 percent ($1 divided by $20).

What purpose does the *back-to-the future yield* serve? It gives you a point of comparison between the stream of income from one stock to another and between stocks and bonds or certificates of deposit.

One of the biggest advantages of stock dividends as compared with other income-bearing investments is that stock dividends tend to increase from year to year while most bonds and CDs stay the same through to maturity.

For instance, if you bought a 4 percent U.S. Treasury Bond 10 years ago, that bond would still be paying the same 4 percent rate.

Compare that with a dividend-paying stock such as Abbott Labs. Abbott stock was selling for about $15 a share in 1994 and paid a dividend of 38 cents. That represented a current yield at the time of about 2.5 percent. But by 2004, Abbott had raised its dividend 10 straight times to $1.05 a share. If you had purchased Abbott in 1994, your current yield based on your original $15 share price would be 7 percent ($1.05 divided by $15). And that *back-to-the-future yield* would continue to climb as long as Abbott Labs continued to grow and raise its dividend.

The *back-to-the-future yield* is included in the profiles of each of the 100 stocks in this book.

Rating the Companies

In selecting the 100 dividend-paying companies for this book, I looked at a wide range of financial factors. The most obvious was the dividend yield—the percentage of return the company pays the shareholder.

But there are some other important factors to consider beyond the yield in selecting dividend-paying stocks for your portfolio. One of those factors is dividend growth. If you rely on dividend income to help cover your basic living expenses, then you may want to avoid companies that rarely raise their dividend. You would be better served to buy stocks that traditionally raise their dividend every year. That way your stream of income would keep pace with inflation or—in many cases—actually exceed the rate of inflation. That's why dividend growth was a critical element in the selection and rating process for this book. I looked for companies that have had strong dividend growth in recent years and that tend to raise their dividend every year (or nearly every year).

The other important factor that is often overlooked by investors interested in high dividend stocks is the financial strength of the company. If the company is weak financially, you could see a drop in the stock price and a drop in the value of your overall portfolio. Companies with weak financials are also less likely to keep raising their dividends, and in some cases, may even lower or eliminate their dividends to make up for short-falls in other areas of their business. For this list, I looked for companies that have experienced solid earnings and revenue growth over the past 10 years.

As a result of this three-phase screening process, the 100 stocks in this book all pay a good dividend—which they tend to raise year in and year out—and they all have a long history of consistent earnings and revenue growth. That means that with these stocks, not only would you receive a good dividend, you would also stand a good chance of seeing your dividend increase each year, and of seeing the overall value of your portfolio increase as the companies grow and the price of their stock appreciates.

As you page through this book, you will see profiles of each of the 100 companies. Accompanying each company profile, you will see a ratings chart similar to the one on the next page.

Rating

Dividend Yield	☆ ☆ ☆ ☆
Dividend Growth	☆ ☆ ☆
Consistency	☆ ☆ ☆
Financial Strength	☆ ☆ ☆
Total	13 Points

This rating system consists of four categories, with a maximum of four points per category—16 points maximum. Each star represents one ratings point.

Following is a breakdown of the scoring for each of the four categories:

Dividend Yield

Yield	Points Awarded
Under 2.5%	No points
2.5 to 2.9%	☆ (1 point)
3.0 to 3.9%	☆ ☆
4.0 to 4.9%	☆ ☆ ☆
5.0% and above	☆ ☆ ☆ ☆

Dividend Growth (Based on rise of the dividend payout over the past five years)

5-Year Growth Rate	Points Awarded
20 to 49%	☆ (1 point)
50 to 74%	☆ ☆
75 to 100%	☆ ☆ ☆
Over 100%	☆ ☆ ☆ ☆

Consistency

A company that has had a flawless run of increases in dividends over the past ten years would score four points. Here is the scoring breakdown:

	Points Awarded
The company has raised its dividend fewer than seven of the past 10 years.	No points
The company has hiked dividends only seven of the past 10 years or at least four years in a row.	☆ (1 point)
The company has increased dividends eight of the past 10 years or at least six years in a row.	☆ ☆
The company has increased dividends nine of the past 10 years or at least eight years in a row.	☆ ☆ ☆
The company posted increased dividends 10 consecutive years or 14 of the past 15 years.	☆ ☆ ☆ ☆

Financial Strength

In order to determine a company's financial strength, I looked at two key areas—earnings growth and revenue growth. Ratings are based on their growth over the past five years. Here is the scoring breakdown:

	Points Awarded
The company increased its earnings less than three of the past five years.	No points
The company increased its earnings at least three of the past five years, but increased its revenue less than three of the past five years.	☆ (1 point)
The company increased its earnings and revenue at least three of the past five years; or the company increased its earnings the past five consecutive years, but increased its revenue less than three of the past five years.	☆ ☆
The company increased both its earnings and revenue at least four of the past five years.	☆ ☆ ☆
The company posted increased earnings and revenue for the past five consecutive years.	☆ ☆ ☆ ☆

Breaking Ties

The 100 companies are ranked in order by points. The company with the most points is ranked first, and the one with the fewest points is ranked 100. To break ties between companies with identical point scores, I looked at several factors, including current yield, the *back-the-future yields*, dividend growth, the company's financial strength, and its growth consistency over the past 10 to 20 years.

How To Use This Book

Think of this book as a shopping catalog for investors. You can page through it, look over the merchandise and make your selections.

Let's assume that you have $100,000 to invest in dividend-bearing stocks. Here is the process I recommend that you use to select the best stocks for you based on the entries in this book:

Begin by reading through the 100 profiles and narrowing your choices to 10 to 15 stocks by asking these questions:

Are they companies you like? Are they involved in business activities that you think have a strong future?

Do they pay a solid dividend, and do they tend to increase that dividend year in and year out?

Do they represent a diverse cross-section of industries? Spread your choices around. You might select a bank, an insurance or investment firm, an energy utility, a real estate investment trust, an oil company, a gas pipeline company, a medical products firm, a consumer products manufacturer, a food company, and a telecommunications operation. Try to choose no more than two or three companies from the same industrial segment. By selecting a broad portfolio, you can minimize your losses if one sector goes sour.

If you wish to use a stockbroker or financial advisor, call your advisor, read your list of choices and ask if he or she has any current research on those stocks. If so, find out which ones the broker recommends, and buy the stocks through your broker.

If you are a do-it-yourself investor, be sure to research the most recent financial information on the stocks you choose to be sure that they still have solid financial fundamentals and still pay an attractive dividend. Not every stock you choose will be a winner, but by selecting a diversified portfolio of solid companies, you can help assure that you will have solid long-term performance and a steadily increasing stream of income.

Here's hoping you can cull from this collection some great stocks that will continue to pay a solid income for many years to come.

BUY

Kinder Morgan Energy Partners

1

500 Dallas Street
Houston, TX 77002
713-369-9000

NYSE: KMP
www.kindermorgan.com

Chairman and CEO: Richard D. Kinder
President: Michael Morgan

Current Yield	6.3%	
Back-to-the-Future Yield	5-year 13.7%	10-year 37.2%

Rating

Dividend Yield	☆ ☆ ☆ ☆ ✓
Dividend Growth	☆ ☆ ☆ ☆
Consistency	☆ ☆ ☆
Financial Strength	☆ ☆ ☆ ☆
Total	15 points

KINDER MORGAN ENERGY PARTNERS IS A MAJOR MOVER IN THE U.S. FUEL market. It owns and operates more than 25,000 miles of pipeline used to transport fuel and natural gas around the country. It is the nation's largest publicly traded pipeline limited partnership and the largest independent refined petroleum products pipeline system in the U.S. in terms of volumes delivered.

Each day, the Houston operation transports more than two million barrels of gasoline, jet fuel, diesel fuel and natural gas liquids through more than 10,000 miles of pipelines. And it moves up to 7.8 billion cubic feet of natural gas through 15,000 miles of pipeline.

The company also operates nearly 100 terminals used to handle over 60 million tons of coal and other dry-bulk materials each year. The firm has a liquids storage capacity of approximately 60 million barrels for petroleum products and chemicals. Kinder Morgan is also the nation's leading provider of CO_2 for enhanced oil recovery projects.

Although Kinder Morgan Energy is a partnership, its stock is publicly traded on the NYSE. The leading shareholder is Kinder Morgan, Inc., which is also a publicly traded company and one of the nation's largest energy transportation and storage companies.

Kinder Morgan Energy has about 1,300 employees and a market capitalization of about $8 billion.

Dividend Yield   ☆ ☆ ☆ ☆
6.3 percent (2004)

Dividend Growth (past five years)   ☆ ☆ ☆ ☆
117 percent

Consistency   ☆ ☆ ☆
Increased dividends seven consecutive years (and eight of the past 10).

Financial Strength   ☆ ☆ ☆ ☆
Increased earnings per share five consecutive years.
Increased revenues five consecutive years.

Financial Summary
Fiscal year ended: Dec. 31

	1998	1999	2000	2001	2002	2003	5-Year Growth (%)
Dividends/share ($)	1.19	1.39	1.60	2.08	2.36	2.58	117
Earnings/share ($)	1.05	1.22	1.34	1.58	1.96	2.00	90
Revenue ($billions)	.32	0.43	.82	2.95	4.24	6.62	1968
Dividend yield (%)	6.8	7.1	7.5	6.1	7.1	6.4	—

5-year stock growth (mid-1999 to mid-2004): 105 percent ($22 to $45)

Thornburg Mortgage, Inc.

2

150 Washington Ave., Suite 302
Santa Fe, NM 87501
505-989-1900

NYSE: TMA
www.thornburgmortgage.com

Chairman and CEO: Garrett Thornburg
President: Larry A. Goldstone

Current Yield	9.1%	
Back-to-the-Future Yield	5-year 27.2%	10-year 20.6%

Rating

Dividend Yield	☆ ☆ ☆ ☆
Dividend Growth	☆ ☆ ☆ ☆
Consistency	☆ ☆
Financial Strength	☆ ☆ ☆
Total	13 points

THORNBURG MORTGAGE IS A REAL ESTATE INVESTMENT TRUST (REIT) THAT focuses on mortgage lending for single family houses. The firm specializes in adjustable rate mortgages (ARMs).

The Santa Fe, New Mexico REIT does direct lending in all 50 states and Washington, D.C. It has built its loan portfolio both by originating mortgage loans and acquiring loans from other mortgage lenders. The company offers mortgages through about 150 correspondent lenders throughout the U.S.

Thornburg generates its profit from the interest spread between the interest income earned on the ARM assets in its portfolio and its financing costs. Because all of its assets are in adjustable rate mortgages, the company contends that it can manage its portfolio successfully through a variety of interest rate environments. To counter the effect of interest rate changes on its borrowing costs, Thornburg tries to closely match the maturities of its borrowings with the repricing of its assets. It also acquires and originates hybrid ARMs with an initial fixed rate period in order to reduce its exposure to mortgage prepayments.

Nearly its entire mortgage portfolio is in AAA and AA-rated or guaranteed government ARM assets.

Founded in 1993, Thornburg has about 76 employees and a stock market capitalization of about $2.3 billion.

Dividend Yield ☆ ☆ ☆ ☆
9.1 percent (2004)

Dividend Growth (past five years) ☆ ☆ ☆ ☆
174 percent

Consistency ☆ ☆
Increased dividends eight of the past 10 years.

Financial Strength ☆ ☆ ☆
Increased earnings five of the past five years.
Increased revenues three of the past five years.

Financial Summary
Fiscal year ended: Dec. 31

	1998	1999	2000	2001	2002	2003	5-Year Growth (%)
Dividends/share ($)	.91	.92	.94	2.00	2.29	2.49	174
Earnings/share ($)	.75	.88	1.05	2.09	2.59	2.71	261
Revenue ($millions)	287	260	290	279	404	598	108
Dividend yield (%)	7.4	10	11.1	13.6	11.6	10.3	—

5-year stock growth (mid-1999 to mid-2004): 180 percent ($10 to $28)

Bank of America

3

Bank of America Corporate Center
100 N. Tryon St.
Charlotte, NC 28255
704-386-5000

NYSE: BAC
www.bankofamerica.com

Chairman, president and CEO: Kenneth D. Lewis

Current Yield	4.1%	
Back-to-the-Future Yield	5-year 5.2%	10-year 12.7%

Rating

Dividend Yield	☆ ☆ ☆
Dividend Growth	☆ ☆ ☆
Consistency	☆ ☆ ☆ ☆
Financial Strength	☆ ☆ ☆
Total	13 points

BANK OF AMERICA WAS CREATED IN 1998 THROUGH THE MERGER OF NationsBank and Bank America. The Charlotte, North Carolina, operation added significantly to its size and clout in 2004 when it completed the acquisition of FleetBoston Financial.

With the addition of FleetBoston, the company has become one of the largest banking organizations in the U.S., with branches on both coasts as well as throughout much of the Southwest and Central U.S.

In all Bank of America has about 5,700 branch offices in 29 states and the District of Columbia, It operates 16,500 ATMs, and boasts about 9 million online banking customers. It also has significant international operations, with offices in 31 countries in Europe, Asia and North and South America, and clients in about 150 countries.

It claims to be the nation's number one small business lender based on number of loans outstanding.

In the lending area, its key areas of business include:

Commercial (26 percent of loans outstanding). The bank provides lending and treasury management services primarily to middle market companies with annual revenues of about $10 million to $500 million.

Commercial real estate (5 percent). The company's commercial real estate lending makes up just a small part of its overall business.

Residential loans (38 percent). The firm is a leading player in the residential mortgage business.

Consumer loans (26 percent). In addition to home mortgages, the company is involved in issuing and servicing credit cards, direct banking, student lending, and insurance services. It also provides financing services for marine, recreational vehicle and auto dealerships.

The bank also provides lending services to its international clients, which accounts for about 5 percent of its total loans outstanding.

Bank of America had about 180,000 employees and a market capitalization of about $117 billion.

Dividend Yield ☆ ☆ ☆
4.1 percent (2004)

Dividend Growth (past five years) ☆ ☆ ☆
81 percent

Consistency ☆ ☆ ☆ ☆
Increased dividends more than 15 consecutive years.

Financial Strength
Increased earnings per share four of the past five years.
Increased assets four of the past five years.

Financial Summary
Fiscal year ended: Dec. 31

	1998	1999	2000	2001	2002	2003	5-Year Growth (%)
Dividends/share ($)	1.59	1.85	2.06	2.28	2.44	2.88	81
Earnings/share ($)	3.64	4.48	4.52	4.18	5.91	7.13	96
Assets ($billions)	58.4	61.7	67.2	65.0	66.2	76.4	31
Dividend yield (%)	2.4	2.9	4.3	4.0	3.6	3.8	—

5-year stock growth (late-1999 to late-2004): 36 percent ($33 to $45)

North Fork Bancorp

4

275 Broad Hollow Road
Melville, NY 11747
613-844-1000

NYSE: NFB
www.northforkbank.com

Chairman, CEO, and President: John A. Kanas

Current Yield	3.3%	
Back-to-the-Future Yield	5-year 5.2%	10-year 23.3%

Rating

Dividend Yield	☆ ☆
Dividend Growth	☆ ☆ ☆ ☆
Consistency	☆ ☆ ☆ ☆
Financial Strength	☆ ☆ ☆
Total	13 points

NORTH FORK BANCORP IS A GROWING REGIONAL BANKING ORGANIZATION operating in the New York City metropolitan area. The company has been growing by acquisition in recent years, snapping up JSB Financial in 2000 and Commercial Bank of New York in 2001. In 2004 it added Trust Company of New Jersey and GreenPoint Financial.

The firm's nearly 200 branch offices all go by the name of North Fork Bank. Its center of operations is the densely populated boroughs of Manhattan, Queens, Brooklyn and the Bronx and the four neighboring New York counties of Nassau, Suffolk, Westchester and Rockland. Its recent acquisitions have given the company an opportunity to branch out into some new territory.

North Fork offers the usual consumer banking services, such as checking, saving, consumer loans, home mortgages, certificates of deposit. It also caters to small and middle level businesses. North Fork also operates two investment management subsidiaries, NFB Investment Services Corp. and Amivest Corp., which offer retail brokerage and investment advisory services to individuals and institutional customers.

North Fork has about 3,000 employees and a market capitalization of about $6 billion.

Dividend Yield ☆ ☆
3.3 percent (2004)

Dividend Growth (past five years) ☆ ☆ ☆ ☆
125 percent

Consistency ☆ ☆ ☆ ☆
Increased dividends 10 consecutive years.

Financial Strength ☆ ☆ ☆
Increased earnings per share four of the past five years.
Increased assets four of the past five years.

Financial Summary
Fiscal year ended: Dec. 31

	1998	1999	2000	2001	2002	2003	5-Year Growth (%)
Dividends/share ($)	0.48	0.60	0.72	0.81	0.98	1.08	125
Earnings/share ($)	1.43	1.52	1.39	2.05	2.58	2.60	82
Assets ($billions)	10.7	13.7	14.8	17.2	21.4	21.0	96
Dividend yield (%)	2.1	2.9	4.1	2.9	2.7	3.1	—

5-year stock growth (late-1999 to late-2004): 95 percent ($22 to $43)

Wells Fargo & Co.

5

420 Montgomery St.
San Francisco, CA 94104
800-292-9932

NYSE: WFC
www.wellsfargo.com

Chairman, CEO and president: Richard M. Kovacevich

Current Yield	3.2%	
Back-to-the-Future Yield	5-year 4.4%	10-year 14.6%

Rating

Dividend Yield	☆ ☆
Dividend Growth	☆ ☆ ☆ ☆
Consistency	☆ ☆ ☆ ☆
Financial Strength	☆ ☆ ☆
Total	13 points

WELLS FARGO IS LONG PAST ITS STAGECOACH DAYS, BUT IT STILL CASTS A long shadow across America. It is the nation's fifth largest banking organization, with about 11 million customers in 23 states. The company has nearly 6,000 locations, including 3,200 bank branches, 830 mortgage offices, and 1,220 consumer finance offices.

Wells Fargo, which merged with Norwest Bank in 1998, is the nation's fifth largest bank. It offers the traditional consumer banking services, as well as investment brokerage and insurance.

The merger between Wells and Norwest is part of a long trend by the two banks. In all, the combined company has been involved in about 1,500 mergers and acquisitions over the past 150 years.

The merged company, based in San Francisco, has carried on part of the philosophy that was the key to Norwest's success prior to the merger. The company refers to its banking offices as "stores," and it approaches the business as a retailer rather than a traditional bank. Its focus is on "cross-selling"—selling multiple services such as savings, checking, CDs, consumer loans, mortgages, credit cards and investment services. A high percentage of its customers use several of its banking services.

Wells Fargo claims to be the national market leader among banks in small business lending, agriculture lending, insurance sales, and prime home equity lending. It offers mortgage services in all 50 states, and boasts about 4 million customers.

Community banking, including insurance and investments, accounts for 70 percent of the company's business. The company also has three other principal divisions, wholesale banking, home mortgages, and consumer finance.

Wells Fargo was founded in 1852 by Henry Wells and William G. Fargo, and is probably best known in Old West folklore as a stage coach operator. The company operated the westernmost leg of the Pony Express and ran stagecoach lines in the Western U.S. The banking business was separated from the express business in 1905.

Wells Fargo has about 140,000 employees and a market capitalization of about $97 billion.

Dividend Yield ☆ ☆
3.2 percent (2004)

Dividend Growth (past five years) ☆ ☆ ☆ ☆
142 percent

Consistency ☆ ☆ ☆ ☆
Increased dividends 17 consecutive years.

Financial Strength ☆ ☆ ☆
Increased earnings per share four of the past five years.
Increased assets more than 10 consecutive years.

Financial Summary
Fiscal year ended: Dec. 31

	1998	1999	2000	2001	2002	2003	5-Year Growth (%)
Dividends/share ($)	0.62	0.79	0.9	1	1.10	1.50	142
Earnings/share ($)	1.75	2.28	2.32	1.97	3.32	3.65	108
Assets ($billions)	202	218	272	308	349	388	92
Dividend yield (%)	1.6	1.9	2.1	2.2	2.3	3.0	—

5-year stock growth (mid-1999 to mid-2004): 48 percent ($40 to $59)

Bank of Nova Scotia

6

Scotia Plaza
44 King St. W.
Toronto, Ontario, Canada M5H 1H1
416-866-6161

TSE: BNS
www.scotiabank.ca

Chairman and CEO: Richard E. Waugh

Current Yield	3.3%	
Back-to-the-Future Yield	5-year 6.2%	10-year 14.5%

Rating

Dividend Yield	☆ ☆
Dividend Growth	☆ ☆ ☆ ☆
Consistency	☆ ☆ ☆ ☆
Financial Strength	☆ ☆ ☆
Total	**13 points**

THE BANK OF NOVA SCOTIA—WHICH, STRANGELY ENOUGH, HAS ITS headquarters far from Nova Scotia in Toronto—may have lost its sense of direction, but it hasn't lost its knack for turning a buck.

The bank has grown steadily throughout the past decade, with nine consecutive years of increased earnings—not bad in a tough Canadian economy. Nor did the bank forget about its shareholders, who have seen their dividends triple since 1996.

The Bank of Nova Scotia is the fourth largest bank in Canada and has a strong international presence. It is the leading provider of financial services in the Caribbean, has a broad network of offices in Asia, and markets its service to the Latin American region through subsidiaries in Chile, Costa Rica, El Salvador and Mexico, and affiliates in Peru and Venezuela. In all, it has nearly

1,900 offices and 3,700 ATMs throughout Canada, the United States and about 45 other countries.

The bank's loan portfolio breaks down this way: commercial loans, 37 percent; real estate and mortgage, 33 percent; personal and other loans, 17 percent; and repurchase agreements, 13 percent.

Founded in 1832, the Bank of Nova Scotia has about 48,000 employees and a market capitalization of about $36 billion (Canadian dollars).

Dividend Yield ☆ ☆
3.3 percent (2004)

Dividend Growth (past five years) ☆ ☆ ☆ ☆
110 percent

Consistency ☆ ☆ ☆ ☆
Increased dividends more than 10 consecutive years.

Financial Strength ☆ ☆ ☆
Increased earnings per share nine consecutive years.
Increased assets three of the past five years.

Financial Summary
Fiscal year ended: Oct. 31
All figures are Canadian Dollars

	1998	1999	2000	2001	2002	2003	5-Year Growth (%)
Dividends/share ($)	.40	.44	.50	.62	.73	.84	110
Earnings/share ($)	1.32	1.47	1.78	2.03	2.20	2.35	78
Assets ($billions)	234	223	253	284	296	286	22
Dividend yield (%)	2.4	2.7	2.9	2.8	2.9	3.0	—

5-year stock growth (mid-1999 to mid-2004): 112 percent ($17 to $36)

U.S. Bancorp

7

800 Nicollet Mall
Minneapolis, MN 55402
651-466-3000

NYSE: USB
www.usbank.com

Chairman, CEO and president: Jerry Grundhofer

Current Yield	3.6%	
Back-to-the-Future Yield	5-year 3.2%	10-year 18.9%

Rating

Dividend Yield	☆ ☆
Dividend Growth	☆ ☆ ☆ ☆
Consistency	☆ ☆ ☆ ☆
Financial Strength	☆ ☆ ☆
Total	13 points

A STEADY DIET OF ACQUISITIONS HAS HELPED U.S. BANCORP BECOME ONE OF the biggest banks in the Midwest and the nation's sixth largest financial services holding company. It acquired Star Bank in 1988, Mercantile Bank in 1999, and made its most significant acquisition in 2001 when it merged with Milwaukee's Firstar Bank.

In all, the Minneapolis-based institution has about 2,300 branch offices and 4,400 ATMs in 24 states.

The bank recently spun off its Piper Jaffray brokerage subsidiary.

U.S. Bancorp offers a broad range of products and services. In addition to checking and savings accounts, brokerage services, and certificates of deposit, U.S. Bank offers consumer loans and credit cards, auto loans, student loans, online banking, and life insurance.

It also offers a full compliment of services for businesses, including business credit cards, employee banking programs and retirement plans, lending and leasing options, lines of credit, investment banking, venture capital, international banking, foreign exchange services, and a variety of merchant services.

The company also provides corporate trust services, such as municipal trusteeships, business escrows, document custody services, international trust services, and money market instruments.

The company has about 51,400 employees and a market capitalization of about $53 billion.

Dividend Yield ☆ ☆
3.6 percent (2004)

Dividend Growth (past five years) ☆ ☆ ☆ ☆
161 percent

Consistency ☆ ☆ ☆ ☆
Increased dividends more than 10 consecutive years.

Financial Strength ☆ ☆ ☆
Increased earnings per share four of the past five years.
Increased assets five of the past five years.

Financial Summary
Fiscal year ended: Dec. 31

	1998	1999	2000	2001	2002	2003	5-Year Growth (%)
Dividends/share ($)	.33	.46	.65	.75	.78	.86	161
Earnings/share ($)	.91	1.25	1.52	1.32	1.84	1.92	111
Assets ($billions)	38.5	72.8	77.6	171.4	180	189	391
Dividend yield (%)	1.5	1.7	2.9	3.4	3.6	3.6	—

5-year stock growth (mid-1999 to mid-2004): 12 percent ($26 to $29)

Synovus Financial

8

One Arsenal Place
901 Front Ave., #301
Columbus, GA 31901
706-649-5220

NYSE: SNV
www.synovus.com

Chairman: James D. Yancey
CEO: James H. Blanchard

Current Yield	2.8%	
Back-to-the-Future Yield	5-year 3.1%	10-year 12.4%

Rating

Dividend Yield	☆
Dividend Growth	☆ ☆ ☆ ☆
Consistency	☆ ☆ ☆ ☆
Financial Strength	☆ ☆ ☆ ☆
Total	13 points

LIKE MANY OF THE NATION'S LARGEST BANKING ORGANIZATIONS, SYNOVUS has grown through a series of acquisitions. But unlike most of its competitors—who typically merge their acquisitions into a single operating unit with a single name—Synvous retains the name of the banks it acquires along with the bank's management team and board of directors. Only the back office duties, such as auditing and data processing are rolled into the home office operations to cut costs.

As a result Synovus operates 39 separate banking organizations, all under different names. If you live in Georgia, Alabama, Florida or South Carolina, where Synvous operates its roughly 200 branch offices, you could be a Synovus Financial customer without even knowing it. For instance, if you do your banking at North Georgia, Citizens Bank of Cochran, The Citizens Bank of Fort Valley, The Bank of Tuscaloosa or the Tallahassee State Bank, you're a customer of Synovus Financial.

The Columbus, Georgia, bank's unique hands-off management strategy has worked well. Synovus has posted 24 consecutive years of record earnings.

In addition to the standard banking services of checking, savings, and money market accounts, Synovus also offers trust services and a full service stock brokerage. Synovus also operates the Synovus Mortgage Corp., which offers mortgage services throughout the Southeast, and Synovus Securities.

It also owns an 81 percent stake in Total System Services, which is one of the world's largest credit, debit and private-label card processing companies. It provides a variety of bankcard and private label credit card data processing services, including card production, international and domestic electronic clearing, cardholder statement preparation, customer service support, merchant accounting and management information and reporting. The company primarily processes cardholder accounts for customers issuing Visa, MasterCard and Diner's Club credit cards along with corporate cards, private label cards and automated teller machine cards.

Founded in 1887, Synovus has about 11,000 employees and a market capitalization of about $7.5 billion.

Dividend Yield
2.8 percent (2004)

Dividend Growth (past five years)
128 percent

Consistency
Increased dividends 24 consecutive years.

Financial Strength
Increased earnings per share 21 consecutive years.
Increased assets more than 10 consecutive years.

Financial Summary
Fiscal year ended: Dec. 31

	1998	1999	2000	2001	2002	2003	5-Year Growth (%)
Dividends/share ($)	0.29	0.36	0.44	0.51	0.59	0.66	128
Earnings/share ($)	0.70	0.80	0.92	1.07	1.23	1.29	84
Assets ($billions)	10.5	12.5	14.9	16.7	19.0	21.6	106
Dividend yield (%)	1.3	1.7	2.2	1.8	2.4	2.9	—

5-year stock growth (late-1999 to late-2004): 23 percent ($22 to $27)

Fifth Third Bancorp

9

38 Fountain Square Plaza
Cincinnati, OH 45263
513-579-5300

NASDAQ: FITB
www.53.com

CEO and President: George A. Schaefer, Jr.

Current Yield	2.6%	
Back-to-the-Future Yield	5-year 2.7%	10-year 12.0%

Rating

Dividend Yield	☆
Dividend Growth	☆ ☆ ☆ ☆
Consistency	☆ ☆ ☆ ☆
Financial Strength	☆ ☆ ☆ ☆
Total	13 points

FIFTH THIRD BANCORP HAS BEEN ONE OF THE NATION'S FASTEST GROWING and most profitable banks over the past two decades. The Cincinnati-based institution operates 17 affiliates with about 1,000 branch offices, including 130 Bank Marts located in supermarkets.

The company also operates a network of 1,844 ATMs in Ohio, Kentucky, Indiana, Michigan, Illinois, Florida, Tennessee and West Virginia.

Fifth Third operates four main businesses segments—retail, commercial, investment advisors and Fifth Third Processing Solutions.

Its loan portfolio breaks down this way: commercial loans, 35 percent; consumer loans, 37 percent; residential mortgages, 8 percent; commercial mortgages, 13 percent; and construction loans, 7 percent.

The company has grown rapidly the past few years through a series of acquisitions, including nearly 50 acquisitions of other financial institutions and related companies. The bank also helped pioneer the use of automatic teller machines (ATM) more than 20 years ago.

Fifth Third's Midwest Payment Systems subsidiary is one of the nation's largest third-party provider of electronic funds transfer services. The subsidiary processes Visa and MasterCard and other credit card transactions for more than 20,000 retail outlets throughout the country.

Fifth Third acquired its improbable-sounding name in the early part of the twentieth century through the merger of the Fifth National and Third National Banks of Ohio.

Founded in 1855, Fifth Third has about 18,563 employees and a market capitalization of about $31 billion.

Dividend Yield ☆
2.6 percent (2004)

Dividend Growth (past five years) ☆ ☆ ☆ ☆
140 percent

Consistency ☆ ☆ ☆ ☆
Increased dividends more than 15 consecutive years.

Financial Strength ☆ ☆ ☆ ☆
Increased earnings per share five of the past five years.
Increased assets five of the past five years.

Financial Summary
Fiscal year ended: Dec. 31

	1998	1999	2000	2001	2002	2003	5-Year Growth (%)
Dividends/share ($)	.47	.59	.70	.83	.98	1.13	140
Earnings/share ($)	1.36	1.61	1.88	2.37	2.76	2.97	118
Assets ($billions)	28.9	41.6	45.9	71	80.9	91.1	215
Dividend yield (%)	1.2	1.3	1.5	1.4	1.5	2.0	—

5-year stock growth (mid-1999 to mid-2004): 17 percent ($41 to $48)

Total S.A.   10

2 place de la Coupole
La Defense 6 92 400
Courbevoie, France
201-626-3090 (U.S.)

NYSE: TOT (trades as an ADR)
www.total.com

Chairman and CEO: Thierry Desmarest

Current Yield	3.3%	
Back-to-the-Future Yield	5-year 8.7%	10-year 18.2%

Rating

Dividend Yield	☆ ☆
Dividend Growth	☆ ☆ ☆ ☆
Consistency	☆ ☆ ☆ ☆
Financial Strength	☆ ☆
Total	12 points

A FRENCH-BASED OIL AND GAS CONGLOMERATE, TOTAL S.A. HAS BEEN ONE of the most consistent performers in the ever-volatile energy industry. The stock, which trades in the U.S. on the New York Stock Exchange as an ADR (American Depository Receipt), has raised its dividends the past 10 consecutive years.

Total was created as the result of a merger between three of Europe's largest gas and oil companies. Total merged with PetroFina in 1998 and Elf Aquitaine in 2000.

In all, the firm has about 18,000 retail service stations throughout the U.S. and Europe.

Total's average daily production level is 1.66 million barrels of crude oil and 4.8 million cubic feet of natural gas.

The company breaks its operations into three key areas:

Upstream includes oil and natural gas exploration and production operations

Downstream involves trading and shipping, refining and marketing of Total, Elf, Fina and Elan petroleum products, automotive and other fuels, and specialties such as aviation fuel and lubricants.

Chemicals include base chemicals and polymers, as well as rubber, resins, adhesives and electroplating.

The company has about 122,000 employees and a market capitalization of about $118 billion.

Dividend Yield ☆ ☆
3.3 percent (2004)

Dividend Growth (past five years) ☆ ☆ ☆ ☆
115 percent

Consistency ☆ ☆ ☆ ☆
Increased dividends 10 consecutive years.

Financial Strength ☆ ☆
Increased earnings per share three of the past five years.
Increased revenue four of the past five years.

Financial Summary
Fiscal year ended: Dec. 31

	1998	1999	2000	2001	2002	2003	5-Year Growth (%)
Dividends/share ($)	1.09	1.10	1.12	1.41	1.74	2.34	115
Earnings/share ($)	2.38	2.40	4.85	4.84	4.24	6.22	161
Revenue ($billions)	27.1	75.5	105.4	93.7	107.7	107.8	298
Dividend yield (%)	1.9	1.8	1.5	2.0	2.4	3.2	—

5-year stock growth (late-1999 to late-2004): 53 percent ($70 to $107)

First Horizon National

11

165 Madison Ave.
Memphis, TN 38103
901-523-4444

NYSE: FHN
www.firsthorizon.com

Chairman and CEO: J. Kenneth Glass

Current Yield	3.8%	
Back-to-the-Future Yield	5-year 3.9%	10-year 13.2%

Rating

Dividend Yield	☆ ☆
Dividend Growth	☆ ☆ ☆
Consistency	☆ ☆ ☆ ☆
Financial Strength	☆ ☆ ☆
Total	12 points

FORMERLY KNOWN AS FIRST TENNESSEE NATIONAL BANK, FIRST HORIZON has expanded well beyond the standard banking services. The Memphis operation offers a wide range of financial services and products through offices in more than 40 states.

The company breaks its operations into three key areas:

First Tennessee Bank. With more than 200 branch offices in Tennessee, Mississippi and Arkansas, First Tennessee is one of the largest banks in the region, offering savings and checking, loans, investments, insurance, financial planning, trust services, asset management, and credit card and cash management services. Its sister bank, First Horizon Bank, operates in the Washington D.C., area.

FTN Financial. FTN offers a broad range of products and services for the investment profession, focusing on the capital markets, equity research, investment banking, correspondent services, and strategic alliances. The company has offices in Boston, Charlotte, Chicago, Cleveland, Dallas, Kansas City, Los Angeles, Memphis, Mobile, Nashville, New York, and Phoenix.

First Horizon. First Horizon Home Loans is one of the nation's 15 largest originators of mortgage loans. First Horizon also offers financial planning, wealth management products, deposit products, and credit cards.

Founded in 1864, First Horizon has about 11,000 employees and a market capitalization of about $5.5 billion.

Dividend Yield ☆ ☆
3.8 percent (2004)

Dividend Growth (past five years) ☆ ☆ ☆
88 percent

Consistency ☆ ☆ ☆ ☆
Increased dividends more than 15 consecutive years.

Financial Strength ☆ ☆ ☆
Increased earnings per share four of the past five years.
Increased assets four of the past five years.

Financial Summary
Fiscal year ended: Dec. 31

	1998	1999	2000	2001	2002	2003	5-Year Growth (%)
Dividends/share ($)	.69	.79	.88	.91	1.05	1.30	88
Earnings/share ($)	1.72	1.85	1.77	2.32	2.89	3.62	110
Assets ($billions)	18.7	18.3	18.6	20.6	23.8	24.5	31
Dividend yield (%)	2.2	2.2	4.1	2.7	2.9	3.1	—

5-year stock growth (mid-1999 to mid-2004): 55 percent ($29 to $45)

Royal Bank of Canada

12

P.O. Box 6001
Montreal, Quebec, Canada H3C 3A9
514-874-2110

NYSE: RY
TSE (Toronto): RY.TO
www.royalbank.com

Chairman and CEO: Gordon Nixon

Current Yield	3.5%	
Back-to-the-Future Yield	5-year 5.6%	10-year 14.0%

Rating

Dividend Yield	☆ ☆
Dividend Growth	☆ ☆ ☆
Consistency	☆ ☆ ☆ ☆
Financial Strength	☆ ☆ ☆
Total	12 points

WITH MORE THAN $400 BILLION (CANADIAN) IN TOTAL ASSETS, THE ROYAL Bank of Canada (RBC) is the nation's largest bank.

The Montreal-based institution has about 1,300 branches and 4,400 ATMs in Canada, and another 800 offices in the U.S. and 30 other foreign countries. In total, the company boasts more than 12 million corporate and individual customers.

RBC has strong presence in the U.S., especially after some recent acquisitions, including Liberty Life Insurance and the Dain Rauscher brokerage.

The bank has a strong home mortgage business, which accounts for about 46 percent of total loans outstanding. Personal loans account for about 20 percent, business, commercial real estate and government loans account for about 32 percent, and credit card loans make up about 2 percent.

RBC ranks first or second among Canadian banks in most commercial and retail services, including mortgages and deposits. It is also the nation's largest securities underwriter and a leading mergers and acquisitions advisor. It is also the nation's largest bank-owned insurer.

RBC was chartered in 1869 as the Merchants' Bank of Halifax. It was renamed the Royal Bank of Canada in 1901. RBC has about 61,000 employees and a market capitalization of about $39 billion.

Dividend Yield ☆ ☆
3.5 percent (2004)

Dividend Growth (past five years) ☆ ☆ ☆
95 percent

Consistency ☆ ☆ ☆ ☆
Increased dividends 10 consecutive years.

Financial Strength ☆ ☆ ☆
Increased earnings per share four of the past five years.
Increased assets four of the past five years.

Financial Summary
Fiscal year ended: Oct. 31
All figures are Canadian Dollars

	1998	1999	2000	2001	2002	2003	5-Year Growth (%)
Dividends/share ($)	.88	.94	1.14	1.38	1.52	1.72	95
Earnings/share ($)	2.65	2.48	3.40	3.55	4.12	4.43	67
Assets ($billions)	274	271	294	362	382	413	51
Dividend yield (%)	2.2	2.7	3.1	2.9	2.9	2.9	—

5-year stock growth (mid-1999 to mid-2004): 109 percent ($22 to $46 U.S. Dollars)

Cedar Fair, L.P.

13

One Cedar Point Drive
Sandusky, OH 44870
419-626-0830

NYSE: FUN
www.cedarfair.com

Chairman, CEO, and President: Richard L. Kinzel

Current Yield	6.0%	
Back-to-the-Future Yield	5-year 8.0%	10-year 11.2%

Rating

Dividend Yield	☆ ☆ ☆ ☆
Dividend Growth	☆
Consistency	☆ ☆ ☆ ☆
Financial Strength	☆ ☆ ☆
Total	12 points

CEDAR FAIR SUMS UP ITS CORPORATE QUEST IN ITS NEW YORK STOCK Exchange Stock symbol: *FUN*. The company operates seven amusement parks and five water parks, mostly in the Midwest.

Its parks include Cedar Point, which is located on Lake Erie between Cleveland and Toledo; Knott's Berry Farm in Buena Park, California, near Los Angeles; Dorney Park & Wildwater Kingdom near Allentown, Pennsylvania; and Geauga Lake, located near Cleveland.

The Sandusky, Ohio, limited partnership also owns Valleyfair near Minneapolis; Worlds of Fun, located in Kansas City, Missouri; and Michigan's Adventure near Muskegon, Michigan.

Cedar Fair's water parks are located near San Diego and in Palm Springs, California, and adjacent to Cedar Point, Knott's Berry Farm and Worlds of Fun.

Cedar Fair also operates Camp Snoopy in the Mall of America in Bloomington, Minnesota under a management contract. Camp Snoopy, which includes a roller coaster, log ride, Ferris wheel and a host of other attractions, is located inside the Mall of America, which is the largest shopping center in the U.S.

Cedar Fair has about 1,400 full-time employees and a market capitalization of about $1.6 billion.

Dividend Yield ☆ ☆ ☆ ☆
6.1 percent (2004)

Dividend Growth (past five years) ☆
37 percent

Consistency ☆ ☆ ☆ ☆
Increased dividends 10 consecutive years.

Financial Strength ☆ ☆ ☆
Increased earnings per share four of the past five years.
Increased revenues 10 consecutive years.

Financial Summary
Fiscal year ended: Dec. 31

	1998	1999	2000	2001	2002	2003	5-Year Growth (%)
Dividends/share ($)	1.27	1.29	1.40	1.50	1.65	1.74	37
Earnings/share ($)	1.48	1.58	1.63	1.36	1.39	1.87	26
Revenue ($millions)	264	420	438	477	503	510	93
Dividend yield (%)	5.8	4.9	6.1	8.0	7.1	6.5	—

5-year stock growth (mid-1999 to mid-2004): 30 percent ($23 to $30)

Associated Banc-Corp.

14

1200 Hansen Road
Green Bay, WI 54307
920-491-7000

NASDAQ: ASBC
www.assocbank.com

Chairman: Robert C. Gallagher
CEO and President: Paul Beideman

Current Yield	3.4%	
Back-to-the-Future Yield	5-year 4.5%	10-year 9.1%

Rating

Dividend Yield	☆ ☆
Dividend Growth	☆ ☆
Consistency	☆ ☆ ☆ ☆
Financial Strength	☆ ☆ ☆ ☆
Total	12 points

ASSOCIATED BANC-CORP. IS A BANK HOLDING COMPANY WITH NEARLY 300 branch offices in Wisconsin, Minnesota and Illinois. The Green Bay-based institution has grown through a series of acquisitions of smaller banking and financial organizations.

In all, the company does business through 22 banking and non-banking subsidiaries.

Associated Banc-Corp. offers a variety of standard banking services, including trust services, asset management and investment services, mortgages, credit and debit cards, personal loans, employee benefit plan management, insurance, cash management services, and savings and checking services.

The company's loan portfolio includes commercial loans (64 percent), residential mortgages (30 percent), and consumer loans (6 percent).

Associated Banc-Corp. was founded in 1970, although many of the branch offices it has acquired in recent years trace their roots to the late 1800s. The company has about 4,200 employees and a market capitalization of $3.2 billion.

Dividend Yield ☆ ☆
3.4 percent (2004)

Dividend Growth (past five years) ☆ ☆
56 percent

Consistency ☆ ☆ ☆ ☆
Increased dividends 32 consecutive years.

Financial Strength ☆ ☆ ☆ ☆
Increased earnings per share five of the past five years.
Increased assets five of the past five years.

Financial Summary
Fiscal year ended: Dec. 31

	1998	1999	2000	2001	2002	2003	5-Year Growth (%)
Dividends/share ($)	.57	.64	.67	.74	.81	.89	56
Earnings/share ($)	1.36	1.42	1.49	1.64	1.86	2.05	51
Assets ($billions)	11.3	12.5	13.1	13.6	15.0	15.2	35
Dividend yield (%)	2.7	3.3	4.4	3.6	3.6	3.6	—

5-year stock growth (mid-1999 to mid-2004): 55 percent ($20 to $31)

SunTrust Banks

15

25 Park Place N.E.
Atlanta, GA 30303
404-588-7711

NYSE: STI
www.suntrust.com

Chairman, CEO, and President: L. Phillip Humann

Current Yield	3.3%	
Back-to-the-Future Yield	5-year 2.7%	10-year 8.0%

Rating

Dividend Yield	☆ ☆
Dividend Growth	☆ ☆ ☆
Consistency	☆ ☆ ☆ ☆
Financial Strength	☆ ☆ ☆
Total	12 points

SUNTRUST BANKS ARE A FAMILIAR SITE THROUGHOUT MUCH OF THE Southeastern United States. The company operates about 1,200 branches and more than 2,200 ATM machines in Florida, Georgia, Tennessee, Virginia, Maryland and Washington, D.C. In all, it has about 3.8 million customers.

The company provides a wide range of personal, corporate and institutional banking services, trust and investment management, investment banking, factoring, mortgage banking, credit cards, discount brokerage, credit-related insurance, and data processing and information services.

Real estate loans account for about 47 percent of the company's outstanding loans, followed by commercial loans, which account for about 38 percent, and consumer loans, which make up 14 percent. Business credit card loans make up just under 1 percent.

SunTrust Banks was created in 1985 with the merger of Sun Banks of Florida and Trust Company of Georgia. It has grown rapidly through a series of acquisitions throughout its four-state operating area.

The company can credit part of its financial strength to an investment it picked up in 1919 as the Trust Company of Georgia. When The Coca-Cola Company went public in 1919, it gave 5,000 shares (worth $110,000) of its stock as part of the underwriting fee to the two underwriters, JP Morgan Bank and the Trust Company of Georgia (now SunTrust Banks). JP Morgan sold its stock, but Trust Company held onto its original shares.

After years of stock splits, that original $110,000 investment is now worth more than $3 billion. Even when the banking business is in a funk, SunTrust continues to ride high on the strength of its Coca-Cola stock.

SunTrust has about 30,000 employees and a market capitalization of about $18 billion.

Dividend Yield
3.3 percent (2004)

Dividend Growth (past five years)
80 percent

Consistency
Increased dividends 26 consecutive years.

Financial Strength
Increased earnings per share four of the past five years.
Increased assets more than 10 consecutive years.

Financial Summary
Fiscal year ended: Dec. 31

	1998	1999	2000	2001	2002	2003	5-Year Growth (%)
Dividends/share ($)	1.00	1.38	1.48	1.60	1.72	1.80	80
Earnings/share ($)	3.04	4.18	4.35	4.78	4.71	4.79	58
Assets ($billions)	93.2	95.4	103.5	104.7	117.3	125.4	35
Dividend yield (%)	1.4	2.0	2.8	2.5	2.7	3.0	—

5-year stock growth (late-1999 to late-2004): -4 percent ($74 to $71)

MBNA Corp.

16

400 Christiana Road
Newark, DE 19713
302-453-9930

NYSE: KRB
www.MBNA.com

Chairman: Randolph D. Lerner
CEO: Bruce Hammonds

Current Yield	2..0%	
Back-to-the-Future Yield	**5-year** 2.6%	**10-year** 15.1%

Rating

Dividend Yield	
Dividend Growth	☆ ☆ ☆ ☆
Consistency	☆ ☆ ☆ ☆
Financial Strength	☆ ☆ ☆ ☆
Total	12 points

MBNA HAS BECOME THE WORLD LARGEST INDEPENDENT CREDIT CARD company by getting to know the people you know. It is the dominant player in the "affinity marketing" credit card segment, issuing specially designed cards endorsed by organizations, universities, associations, and other groups.

In other words, when you get a solicitation from MBNA, it's not just any junk mail—it's junk mail from your alma mater, your club, your favorite sports team, or even your favorite charity or environmental group. Belong to the National Audubon Society? MBNA has a card for you. Got a favorite NBA basketball team? There's a card for them, as well.

In all, MBNA has more than 50 million credit card customers, and associations with about 5,100 organizations.

Under the affinity group arrangement, MBNA gives the endorsing group a small percentage of the profits on all the transactions registered on the cards sold through that association—a fact that is built into the marketing campaign to encourage customers to sign up. The cards issued to affinity group members usually carry custom graphics and the name and logo of the endorsing organization.

The Wilmington, Delaware firm has operations in Canada, Ireland, Spain, and the United Kingdom.

The company has about 29,000 employees and a market capitalization of about $30 billion.

Dividend Yield
2.0 percent (2004)

Dividend Growth (past five years)   ☆ ☆ ☆ ☆
140 percent

Consistency   ☆ ☆ ☆ ☆
Increased dividends 10 consecutive years.

Financial Strength   ☆ ☆ ☆ ☆
Increased earnings per share five of the past five years.
Increased assets five of the past five years.

Financial Summary
Fiscal year ended: Dec. 31

	1998	1999	2000	2001	2002	2003	5-Year Growth (%)
Dividends/share ($)	.15	.18	.21	.23	.27	.36	140
Earnings/share ($)	.65	.81	1.02	1.28	1.47	1.79	175
Assets ($billions)	72	85.5	108	118	131	144	100
Dividend yield (%)	1.1	1.0	1.0	1.0	1.2	1.7	—

5-year stock growth (mid-1999 to mid-2004): 50 percent ($16 to $24)

Duke Realty Corp.

17

600 E. 96th St., Suite 100
Indianapolis, IN 46240
317-808-6000

NYSE: DRE
www.dukerealty.com

Chairman: Thomas L. Hefner
President and CEO: Dennis D. Oklak

Current Yield	5.7%	
Back-to-the-Future Yield	5-year 9.0%	10-year 15.3%

Rating

Dividend Yield	☆ ☆ ☆ ☆
Dividend Growth	☆
Consistency	☆ ☆ ☆ ☆
Financial Strength	☆ ☆
Total	11 points

DUKE REALTY OWNS A BROAD PORTFOLIO OF REAL ESTATE PROPERTIES THAT is diversified by both type and location. The Indianapolis-based real estate investment trust (REIT) owns and operates industrial, office and retail buildings in 13 U.S. cities, primarily in the Midwest and Southeast..

In all, Duke owns and operates about 900 properties encompassing more than 118 million square feet of building space. It also owns about 3,900 acres of undeveloped land that could be developed later. The company has a total market capitalization (real estate properties) of about $8 billion.

Duke also offers a fee-based service for other property owners that provides leasing, property and asset management, development, construction, build-to-suit, and other tenant-related services. In all, the company provides services for about 300 fee-based tenants.

Founded in 1972, Duke had its initial public offering in 1986. The firm has about 1,400 employees and a stock market capitalization of about $4.6 billion.

Dividend Yield ☆ ☆ ☆ ☆
5.7 percent (2004)

Dividend Growth (past five years) ☆
43 percent

Consistency ☆ ☆ ☆ ☆
Increased dividends 10 consecutive years.

Financial Strength ☆ ☆
Increased earnings per share three of the past five years.
Increased revenues four of the past five years.

Financial Summary
Fiscal year ended: Dec. 31

	1998	1999	2000	2001	2002	2003	5-Year Growth (%)
Dividends/share ($)	1.28	1.46	1.64	1.76	1.81	1.83	43
Earnings/share ($)	1.12	1.32	1.66	1.75	1.19	1.19	6
Revenue ($millions)	373	590	795	804	780	790	112
Dividend yield (%)	5.6	7.1	7.6	7.4	7.2	6.7	—

5-year stock growth (mid-1999 to mid-2004): 57 percent ($21 to $33)

Teppco Partners, L.P.

18

2929 Allen Pkwy
P.O. Box 2521
Houston, TX 77252
713-759-3636

NYSE: TPP
www.teppco.com

Chairman and CEO: Jim Mogg

Current Yield	7.0%	
Back-to-the-Future Yield	5-year 11.4%	10-year 18.8%

Rating

Dividend Yield	☆ ☆ ☆ ☆
Dividend Growth	☆ ☆
Consistency	☆ ☆ ☆ ☆
Financial Strength	☆
Total	11 points

TEPPCO PARTNERS OPERATES ONE OF THE NATION'S LARGEST FUEL PIPELINE networks. In all, it operates about 11,600 miles of pipeline used to transport crude oil, liquefied petroleum gas, natural gas, natural gas liquids, and petrochemicals.

The company's pipelines cover much of Texas and run up through the South, the Midwest and into the New England area.

The Houston-based operation is a limited partnership that trades as a stock on the NYSE. Teppco operates in three primary segments, including refined petroleum products, liquefied petroleum gases, and petrochemical transportation and storage.

Founded in 1990, Teppco has grown rapidly through a series of acquisitions. It owns a 50 percent stake in Seaway Crude Pipeline Company and Centennial Pipeline. It also owns an undivided ownership interest in the Basin Pipeline.

In 2003, Teppco formed Mont Belvieu Storage Partners, a joint venture between Teppco and Louis Dreyfus Energy Services. It also acquired crude supply and transportation assets along the upper Texas Gulf Coast from Genesis Pipeline Texas.

Teppco Partners has about 1,000 employees and a market capitalization of about $2.4 billion.

Dividend Yield   ☆ ☆ ☆ ☆
7.0 percent (2004)

Dividend Growth (past five years)   ☆ ☆
43 percent

Consistency   ☆ ☆ ☆ ☆
Increased dividends 11 consecutive years.

Financial Strength   ☆
Increased earnings per share only two of the past five years.
Increased revenue 10 consecutive years.

Financial Summary
Fiscal year ended: Dec. 31

	1998	1999	2000	2001	2002	2003	5-Year Growth (%)
Dividends/share ($)	1.75	1.85	2.00	2.15	2.35	2.50	43
Earnings/share ($)	1.61	1.91	1.89	2.18	1.79	1.52	—
Revenue ($billions)	.43	1.93	3.09	3.56	3.24	4.26	891
Dividend yield (%)	6.3	7.8	8.7	7.3	7.8	7.2	—

5-year stock growth (late-1999 to late-2004): 86 percent ($21 to $39)

Kimco Realty Corp.   19

3333 New Hyde Park Road
New Hyde Park, NY 11042
516-869-9000

NYSE: KIM
www.kimcorealty.com

Chairman and CEO: Milton Cooper

Current Yield	5.1%	
Back-to-the-Future Yield	5-year 9.4%	10-year 14.1%

Rating

Dividend Yield	☆ ☆ ☆ ☆
Dividend Growth	☆
Consistency	☆ ☆ ☆
Financial Strength	☆ ☆ ☆
Total	11 points

KIMCO IS A REAL ESTATE INVESTMENT TRUST (REIT) THAT HAS BEEN specializing in neighborhood and community shopping centers for more than 40 years. In fact, it is the nation's largest publicly traded owner and operator of neighborhood and community shopping centers.

The New Hyde Park, New York REIT has about 700 properties throughout the U.S. In all, it owns and operates about 100 million square feet of leasable space.

Among its largest tenants are Home Depot (3 percent of revenues), Kmart (2.9 percent), Kohl's (2.8 percent), and Royal Ahold (2.6 percent).

Kimco owns and operates about 620 neighborhood and community shopping centers, 36 retail stores, 33 "ground-up developments," and 10 parcels of undeveloped land. The company has properties in 41 states, Canada and Mexico.

Founded in 1960, Kimco has about 400 employees and a stock market capitalization of about $5.3 billion.

Dividend Yield   ☆ ☆ ☆ ☆
5.0 percent (2004)

Dividend Growth (past five years)   ☆
32 percent

Consistency   ☆ ☆ ☆
Increased dividends nine of the past 10 years.

Financial Strength   ☆ ☆ ☆
Increased earnings four of the past five years.
Increased revenues five of the past five years.

Financial Summary
Fiscal year ended: Dec. 31

	1998	1999	2000	2001	2002	2003	5-Year Growth (%)
Dividends/share ($)	1.66	1.60	1.81	1.96	2.10	2.19	32
Earnings/share ($)	1.35	1.64	1.91	2.16	2.16	2.21	64
Revenue ($millions)	330	401	423	431	432	480	45
Dividend yield (%)	5.3	6.6	6.9	6.4	6.9	5.7	—

5-year stock growth (mid-1999 to mid-2004): 100 percent ($25 to $50)

Archstone-Smith Trust

20

9200 E. Panorama Circle, Suite 400
Englewood, CO 80112
303-708-5959

NYSE: ASN
www.archstonesmith.com

Chairman and CEO: R. Scott Sellers

Current Yield	6.5%	
Back-to-the-Future Yield	5-year 8.1%	10-year 9.2%

Rating

Dividend Yield	☆ ☆ ☆ ☆
Dividend Growth	☆
Consistency	☆ ☆ ☆ ☆
Financial Strength	☆ ☆
Total	**11 points**

ARCHSTONE-SMITH IS A REAL ESTATE INVESTMENT TRUST (REIT) THAT focuses primarily on multi-family housing. The company, in its present form, was formed in 2001 through the merger of Archstone Community Trust and Smith Residential Trust.

In all, the company owns and operates about 88,000 units (including some that are still in the planning and construction phase).

Most of Archtone's properties are high-rise and garden apartment complexes located in affluent neighborhoods in the greater Washington, D.C. metropolitan area, Southern California, the San Francisco Bay area, Chicago, Boston, southeast Florida, Seattle and the greater New York City metropolitan area. Its largest concentration of housing is in the Washington, D.C. area, which accounts for about 40 percent of its total units.

The company does business through several real estate arms. Archstone Communities operates garden-style apartments throughout the country. Charles E. Smith Residential operates upscale high-rise apartment buildings in Washington, D.C., Chicago, Boston and Southeast Florida. Ameriton Properties focuses on the acquisition, development and sale of apartment complexes. Smith Corporate Living provides furnished apartments for corporate customers who need long-term accommodations.

In all, the company owns about 250 complexes

Archstone-Smith has a market capitalization of about $6 billion.

Dividend Yield
6.5 percent (2004)

Dividend Growth (past five years)
23 percent

Consistency
Increased dividends 10 consecutive years.

Financial Strength
Increased earnings per share three of the past five years.
Increased revenues four of the past five years.

Financial Summary
Fiscal year ended: Dec. 31

	1998	1999	2000	2001	2002	2003	5-Year Growth (%)
Dividends/share ($)	1.39	1.48	1.54	1.64	1.70	1.71	23
Earnings/share ($)	.98	1.02	1.20	1.06	1.39	1.22	24
Revenue ($millions)	484	553	585	556	862	900	86
Dividend yield (%)	6.6	7.0	6.7	6.5	6.7	7.0	—

5-year stock growth (mid-1999 to mid-2004): 48 percent ($21 to $31)

BB&T Corp.

200 West 2nd St.
Winston-Salem, NC
910-272-2273

NYSE: BBT
www.BBandT.com

Chairman and CEO: John A. Allison IV

Current Yield	3.5%	
Back-to-the-Future Yield	5-year 3.8%	10-year 13%

Rating

Dividend Yield	☆ ☆
Dividend Growth	☆ ☆ ☆
Consistency	☆ ☆ ☆ ☆
Financial Strength	☆ ☆
Total	11 points

BB&T, (FORMERLY BRANCH BANKING AND TRUST) HAS BECOME ONE OF THE largest banking organizations in the Southeast through a series of acquisitions in 11 states and the District of Columbia.

The Winston-Salem, North Carolina institution has more than 1,100 branch offices in North and South Carolina, Virginia, Maryland, Georgia, Tennessee, West Virginia, Alabama, Kentucky, Indiana, Florida and Washington, D.C. The largest concentration of branches is in Virginia, with 427 branches, and its home state of North Carolina, with about 333 offices.

In all, the company has acquired 58 banks and thrifts, 66 insurance agencies and 22 non-bank financial services firms in the past 15 years.

BB&T offers a wide range of services, including small business lending, commercial middle market lending, real estate lending, retail lending, home equity and mortgage lending, sales finance, leasing, asset management, and trust services.

It also offers agency insurance, treasury services, investment and mutual fund sales, capital markets, factoring, asset-based lending, international banking services, cash management, electronic payment services, credit and debit card services, and payroll processing.

BB&T also operates Scott & Stringfellow, a broker-dealer in Richmond, Virginia, with more than 40 full-service retail brokerage offices in Virginia, North Carolina and South Carolina.

The company's loan portfolio breaks down this way: mortgages, 58 percent; commercial, 12 percent; consumer, 15 percent; and construction, 15 percent.

The company's commercial lending program is targeted to small and mid-sized companies with sales of $200 million or less. It also offers a number of construction loans for new homes and commercial buildings, including industrial facilities, apartments, shopping centers, office buildings, hotels, and warehouses.

Founded in 1872, BB&T is the oldest bank headquartered in North Carolina. BB&T has about 28,300 full-time equivalent employees and a market capitalization of about $19 billion.

Dividend Yield ☆ ☆
3.5 percent (2004)

Dividend Growth (past five years) ☆ ☆ ☆
85 percent

Consistency ☆ ☆ ☆ ☆
Increased dividends more than 10 consecutive years.

Financial Strength ☆ ☆
Increased earnings per share three of the past five years.
Increased assets more than five consecutive years.

Financial Summary

Fiscal year ended: Dec. 31

	1998	1999	2000	2001	2002	2003	5-Year Growth (%)
Dividends/share ($)	0.66	0.75	0.86	0.98	1.10	1.22	85
Earnings/share ($)	1.60	1.71	1.53	2.12	2.70	2.07	29
Assets ($billions)	54.4	59.4	66.6	70.9	80.2	90.5	66
Dividend yield (%)	2.0	2.1	3.1	2.7	3.0	3.5	—

5-year stock growth (mid-1999 to mid-2004): 53 percent ($32 to $40)

AmSouth Bancorp

22

P.O. Box 11007
Birmingham, AL 35288
205-320-7151

NYSE: ASO
www.amsouth.com

Chairman, CEO, and President: C. Dowd Ritter

Current Yield	4.2%	
Back-to-the-Future Yield	5-year 3.5%	10-year 10.6%

Rating

Dividend Yield	☆ ☆ ☆
Dividend Growth	☆ ☆
Consistency	☆ ☆ ☆ ☆
Financial Strength	☆ ☆
Total	11 points

AMSOUTH BANCORP IS THE NATION'S 21ST LARGEST BANKING ORGANIZATION, based on total assets.

The Birmingham, Alabama operation provides banking services at about 650 branch offices located in Alabama, Florida, Tennessee, Mississippi, Louisiana and Georgia. The firm also operates a network of more than 1,200 automated teller machines that are linked with shared automated tellers in all 50 states.

The company breaks its operations into three key segments:

Consumer banking. Consumer loans account for about 52 percent of total loans outstanding. The bank offers a full range of financial services to individuals and small businesses, including checking and savings accounts, and loan services such as residential mortgages, equity lending, credit cards, and loans for automobile and other personal financing needs. It also offers similar products and services for small businesses.

Commercial banking. Commercial loans and commercial real estate loans account for about 48 percent of total loans outstanding. The bank offers a variety of products and services for large and middle market corporate customers, including credit, treasury management, international and capital markets services. Those services include several specialty areas such as real estate finance, asset based lending and commercial leasing.

Wealth Management. The firm offers trust, institutional, retirement and broker-dealer services, including traditional trust, custody and agency services as well as investment management services.

Founded in 1970, AmSouth has about 12,385 full-time equivalent employees and a market capitalization of about $8 billion.

Dividend Yield ☆ ☆ ☆
4.2 percent (2004)

Dividend Growth (past five years) ☆ ☆
64 percent

Consistency ☆ ☆ ☆ ☆
Increased dividends more than 10 consecutive years.

Financial Strength ☆ ☆
Increased earnings per share three of the past five years.
Increased assets three of the past five years.

Financial Summary
Fiscal year ended: Dec. 31

	1998	1999	2000	2001	2002	2003	5-Year Growth (%)
Dividends/share ($)	0.56	0.70	0.80	0.84	0.88	0.92	64
Earnings/share ($)	1.22	0.87	0.86	1.46	1.70	1.79	47
Assets ($billions)	40.6	43.4	38.9	38.6	40.6	45.6	12
Dividend yield (%)	2.2	2.7	5.1	4.8	4.2	4.3	—

5-year stock growth (mid-1999 to mid-2004): 0 percent ($25 to $25)

Weingarten Realty Investors

2600 Citadel Plaza Drive
P.O. Box 924133
Houston, TX 77292
713-866-6000

NYSE: WRI
www.weingarten.com

Chairman: Stanford Alexander
President: Andrew M. Alexander

Current Yield	5.1%	
Back-to-the-Future Yield	5-year 8.6%	10-year 9.8%

Rating

Dividend Yield	☆ ☆ ☆ ☆
Dividend Growth	☆
Consistency	☆ ☆ ☆
Financial Strength	☆ ☆ ☆
Total	11 points

FOR MORE THAN 50 YEARS, WEINGARTEN REALTY HAS BEEN ACQUIRING A broad portfolio of neighborhood and community shopping centers. The Houston-based real estate investment trust (REIT) owns (or has ownership interests) in about 280 shopping centers in 20 Southern and Western states.

Most of the company's properties are relatively small neighborhood centers anchored by a grocery store, drug store, book store or similar high volume retailer.

Weingarten also owns 62 industrial facilities in six states. Its total real estate market capitalization is about $5 billion.

About 90 percent of the company's rental income is generated by shopping centers. Industrial tenants account for the other 10 percent. In the future, the company plans to focus almost entirely on community shopping centers.

Founded in 1948, Weingarten became a REIT and a publicly traded stock in 1985. The company has 309 employees and a stock market capitalization of about $2.8 billion.

Dividend Yield ☆ ☆ ☆ ☆
5.1 percent (2004)

Dividend Growth (past five years) ☆
30 percent

Consistency ☆ ☆ ☆
Increased dividends eight consecutive years.

Financial Strength ☆ ☆ ☆
Increased earnings four of the past five years.
Increased revenues five of the past five years.

Financial Summary
Fiscal year ended: Dec. 31

	1998	1999	2000	2001	2002	2003	5-Year Growth (%)
Dividends/share ($)	1.20	1.26	1.33	1.41	1.48	1.56	30
Earnings/share ($)	.90	.93	.99	1.11	1.19	1.16	29
Revenue ($millions)	199	230	273	320	372	419	111
Dividend yield (%)	7.4	10	11.1	13.6	11.6	10.3	—

5-year stock growth (mid-1999 to mid-2004): 78 percent ($18 to $32)

Peoples Energy Corp.

24

130 E. Randolph Dr.
Chicago, IL 60601
312-240-4000

NYSE: PGL
www.pecorp.com

Chairman and CEO: Thomas M. Patrick

Current Yield	5.1%	
Back-to-the-Future Yield	5-year 5.9%	10-year 7.9%

Rating

Dividend Yield	☆ ☆ ☆ ☆
Dividend Growth	
Consistency	☆ ☆ ☆ ☆
Financial Strength	☆ ☆ ☆
Total	11 points

PEOPLES ENERGY IS CHICAGO'S OLDEST UTILITY. FOUNDED IN 1848, PEOPLES lit up Chicago with natural gas for its street lights beginning in 1850.

More than 150 years later, the company still provides natural gas for more than a million customers in the greater Chicago area. It operates about 6,500 miles of gas line. The utility serves both residential and business customers.

Peoples also has its hands in some other energy-related areas. It operates some power generators in the Chicago area and other markets. It also owns a Houston-based subsidiary that acquires and develops onshore oil and gas properties with proven reserves. Its properties are located in Texas, Louisiana and New Mexico.

Peoples Energy has about 2,400 employees and a market capitalization of about $1.6 million.

Dividend Yield

5.1 percent (2004)

Dividend Growth (past five years)

11 percent

Consistency

☆ ☆ ☆ ☆

Increased its dividend 14 out of the past 15 years.

Financial Strength

☆ ☆ ☆

Increased earnings per share four of the past five years.
Increased revenue four of the past five years.

Financial Summary

Fiscal year ended: Sept. 30

	1998	1999	2000	2001	2002	2003	5-Year Growth (%)
Dividends/share ($)	1.91	1.95	1.99	2.03	2.07	2.11	11
Earnings/share ($)	2.25	2.52	2.34	2.74	2.51	2.87	28
Revenue ($billions)	1.13	1.19	1.42	2.27	1.48	2.14	88
Dividend yield (%)	5.2	5.3	6.1	5.2	5.5	5.5	—

5-year stock growth (late-1999 to late-2004): 13 percent ($39 to $44)

Regions Financial Corp.

25

417 N. 20th St.
Birmingham, AL 35203
205-944-1300

NYSE: RF
www.regionsbank.com

Chairman, CEO, and President: Carl E. Jones, Jr.

Current Yield	4.6%	
Back-to-the-Future Yield	5-year 4.1%	10-year 8.1%

Rating

Dividend Yield	☆ ☆ ☆
Dividend Growth	☆
Consistency	☆ ☆ ☆ ☆
Financial Strength	☆ ☆ ☆
Total	11 points

REGIONS FINANCIAL, AN ALABAMA-BASED BANKING ORGANIZATION, NEARLY doubled its size in 2004 with the acquisition of Memphis-based Union Planters Corp. The combined operation has about $80 billion in assets and five million customers in a 15-state area throughout the South, Midwest and Texas. It has about 1,400 branch offices and a network of about 1,700 ATM machines.

Regions offers the typical retail banking services, such as savings and checking accounts, certificates of deposit, trust services, consumer loans, and home mortgages. The institution also offers a wide range of commercial banking services. Through its subsidiaries, Regions also offers securities brokerage services and insurance products.

The company provides investment and brokerage services through its Morgan Keegan & Company subsidiary, which is one of the largest investment banking firms in the South with more than $30 billion in assets under management.

Regions acquired Morgan Keegan in 2001. The same year, Regions also acquired Rebsamen Insurance, Inc., which offers a full-line of insurance products, primarily focusing on commercial property and casualty insurance customers.

Regions Financial was formed in 1971 as First Alabama Bancshares Inc. It was renamed Regions Financial Corp. in 1994.

Regions has about 25,000 employees and a market capitalization of about $14 billion.

Dividend Yield ☆ ☆ ☆
4.6 percent (2004)

Dividend Growth (past five years) ☆
35 percent

Consistency ☆ ☆ ☆ ☆
Increased dividends 33 consecutive years.

Financial Strength ☆ ☆ ☆
Increased earnings per share four of the past five years.
Increased assets more than 10 consecutive years.

Financial Summary
Fiscal year ended: Dec. 31
(Table represents Region's figures prior to its merger with Union Planters)

	1998	1999	2000	2001	2002	2003	5-Year Growth (%)
Dividends/share ($)	0.92	1.00	1.08	1.11	1.16	1.24	35
Earnings/share ($)	1.88	2.35	2.38	2.24	2.72	2.90	54
Assets ($billions)	36.8	42.7	43.7	45.4	47.9	48.6	32
Dividend yield (%)	2.3	2.9	4.8	3.7	3.5	3.6	—

5-year stock growth (mid-1999 to mid-2004): 32 percent ($25 to $33)

Jefferson-Pilot Corp.

100 North Green St.
Greensboro, NC 27401
336-691-3000

NYSE: JP
www.jpfinancial.com

Chairman: David A. Stonecipher
President and CEO: Dennis R. Glass

Current Yield	3.1%	
Back-to-the-Future Yield	5-year 3.0%	10-year 14.3%

Rating

Dividend Yield	☆ ☆
Dividend Growth	☆ ☆
Consistency	☆ ☆ ☆ ☆
Financial Strength	☆ ☆ ☆
Total	11 points

JEFFERSON PILOT MAY BE BEST KNOWN FOR ITS LINE OF INSURANCE AND annuity products, but it has also established a sizable presence in America's airwaves.

The Greensboro, North Carolina operation owns and operates three network television stations and 17 radio stations. It owns television stations in Charleston, South Carolina, Charlotte, North Carolina, and Richmond Virginia, and radio stations in Atlanta, Charlotte, Denver, Miami and San Diego. The communications division, which also produces television sports programs covering college basketball and football and professional motor sports, accounts for about 9 percent of Jefferson-Pilot's total revenue.

The remainder of the company's revenue comes from its insurance and investment groups. Through its Jefferson-Pilot and Alexander Hamilton life insurance companies, the company offers continuous and limited-pay life and endowment policies, universal life policies, retirement income plans, and level and decreasing term insurance. Life insurance products account for about 59 percent of the company's operating income.

Jefferson-Pilot also offers a range of investment products and services, including several types of annuities and mutual funds. Annuities and investment products generate about 16 percent of operating income. Other operations, such as benefit partners and corporate services and investments make up the other 16 percent.

The company's life insurance and investment products are sold through a nationwide network of more than 2,300 independent agents.

Founded in 1890, Jefferson-Pilot has about 4,000 employees and a market capitalization of about $6.7 billion.

Dividend Yield ☆ ☆
3.1 percent (2004)

Dividend Growth (past five years) ☆ ☆
68 percent

Consistency ☆ ☆ ☆ ☆
Increased dividends 23 consecutive years.

Financial Strength ☆ ☆ ☆
Increased earnings per share four of the past five years.
Increased revenues four of the past five years.

Financial Summary
Fiscal year ended: Dec. 31

	1998	1999	2000	2001	2002	2003	5-Year Growth (%)
Dividends/share ($)	.77	.86	.96	1.07	1.18	1.29	68
Earnings/share ($)	2.61	2.95	2.85	3.06	3.14	3.66	40
Income ($billions)	2.56	2.46	3.14	3.26	3.50	3.62	41
Dividend yield (%)	1.9	1.9	2.3	2.4	2.7	3.0	—

5-year stock growth (mid-1999 to mid-2004): 12 percent ($43 to $48)

Peoples Bank 27

850 Main St.
Bridgeport, CT 06604
203-338-7171

Nasdaq: PBCT
www.peoples.com

Chairman, president and CEO: John A. Klein

Current Yield	3.6%	
Back-to-the-Future Yield	5-year 6.3%	10-year 19.4%

Rating

Dividend Yield	☆ ☆
Dividend Growth	☆ ☆ ☆
Consistency	☆ ☆ ☆ ☆
Financial Strength	☆ ☆
Total	11 points

FOUNDED IN 1842, PEOPLE'S BANK IS THE LARGEST STATE-CHARTERED BANK in Connecticut. The Bridgeport institution is a dominant player in its home market, boasting business relationships with more than 25 percent of households in Connecticut.

The bank has about 150 branches throughout the state, as well as 60 seven-day-a-week offices in Super Stop & Shop stores.

People's provides the standard consumer and commercial financial services, such as checking, savings, consumer and small business loans and mortgages. It also offers brokerage and advisory services, asset management, insurance services and equipment leasing and financing. Its subsidiaries include People's Securities, Olson Mobeck Investment Advisors, RC Knox & Company and People's Capital and Leasing Corp. People's is the top issuer of Savings Bank Life Insurance in the state.

People's converted to a mutual holding company with public ownership in 1988.

People's was the first financial institution in the nation to offer bill paying by phone in 1974. It was also the first bank in the region to open supermarket branches.

People's has about 3,800 employees and a market capitalization of about $3 billion.

Dividend Yield ☆ ☆
3.6 percent (2004)

Dividend Growth (past five years) ☆ ☆ ☆
82 percent

Consistency ☆ ☆ ☆ ☆
Increased dividends 10 consecutive years.

Financial Strength ☆ ☆
Increased earnings per share three of the past five years.
Increased assets four of the past five years.

Financial Summary
Fiscal year ended: Dec. 31

	1998	1999	2000	2001	2002	2003	5-Year Growth (%)
Dividends/share ($)	.56	.69	.80	.89	.95	1.02	82
Earnings/share ($)	1.04	1.21	1.18	.26	.60	.69	—
Assets ($billions)	9.9	10.7	11.6	11.9	12.3	11.7	18
Dividend yield (%)	2.6	3.8	5.9	5.6	5.8	5.3	—

5-year stock growth (late-1999 to late-2004): 138 percent ($16 to $38)

Astoria Financial Corp.

28

One Astoria Federal Plaza
Lake Success, NY 11042
516-327-3000

NYSE: AF
www.asfc.com

Chairman, CEO, and President: George L. Engelke, Jr.

Current Yield	2.8%	
Back-to-the-Future Yield	5-year 4.7%	10-year 12.5%

Rating

Dividend Yield	☆
Dividend Growth	☆ ☆ ☆ ☆
Consistency	☆ ☆ ☆ ☆
Financial Strength	☆ ☆
Total	11 points

ASTORIA FEDERAL IS A SAVINGS AND LOAN ASSOCIATION IN THE NEW YORK City area, with about 86 branches and 120 ATM locations in the Long Island counties of Brooklyn, Queens, Nassau, and Suffolk, as well as neighboring Westchester County.

Founded in 1888, Astoria is the nation's sixth largest thrift, and the third largest in New York. It offers the standard consumer banking services, such as checking, savings, consumer lending, financial services, and small business loans. The firm has about 700,000 customers.

Astoria also originates mortgage loans through a network of brokers in 19 states, primarily on the East Coast. It also has correspondent relationships for mortgage business in 44 states.

Family mortgages account for about 71 percent of its loan portfolio, multi-family loans make up 18 percent, real estates comprises 7 percent, and consumer and other loans makes up 4 percent.

Astoria has acquired three smaller New York area thrifts since 1998. The firm has about 3,820 employees and a market capitalization of about $2.8 billion.

Dividend Yield ☆
2.8 percent (2004)

Dividend Growth (past five years) ☆ ☆ ☆ ☆
115 percent

Consistency ☆ ☆ ☆ ☆
Increased dividends 8 consecutive years.

Financial Strength ☆ ☆
Increased earnings per share four of the past five years.
Increased assets three of the past five years.

Financial Summary
Fiscal year ended: Dec. 31

	1998	1999	2000	2001	2002	2003	5-Year Growth (%)
Dividends/share ($)	.40	.48	.51	.61	.77	.86	115
Earnings/share ($)	1.32	2.04	2.16	2.38	2.85	2.49	87
Assets ($billions)	20.6	22.7	22.3	22.7	21.7	22.5	9
Dividend yield (%)	1.6	2.4	3.2	2.2	2.6	3.0	—

5-year stock growth (late-1999 to late-2004): 105 percent ($19 to $39)

ConAgra Foods, Inc.

One ConAgra Drive
Omaha, NE 68102
402-595-4000

NYSE: CAG
www.conagra.com

Chairman, CEO, and President: Bruce Rohde

Current Yield	3.9%	
Back-to-the-Future Yield	5-year 5.1%	10-year 7.1%

Rating

Dividend Yield	☆ ☆ ☆
Dividend Growth	☆ ☆
Consistency	☆ ☆ ☆ ☆
Financial Strength	☆ ☆
Total	11 points

CONAGRA SERVES UP A VERITABLE BUFFET OF FOODS AND MEATS. IT IS ONE of the world's largest food production companies.

The Omaha-based operation produces products for several food categories, including:

> **Stable shelf products**. ConAgra produces canned tomatoes, cooking oils, popcorn, soup, puddings, meat snacks, canned beans, canned pasta, canned chili, cocoa mixes and peanut butter. Its leading brands include Hunts, Healthy Choice, Chef Boyardee, Wesson, Orville Redenbacher's, PAM, Slim Jim, ACT II, Peter Pan, Van Camp's, Gulden's, Beanee Weenee, Manwich, Hunt's Snack Pack, Swiss Miss, Knott's Berry Farm, La Choy, Gebhardt, DAVID, Wolf Brand, Pemmican, Penrose and Andy Capp's.

Frozen foods. ConAgra makes pizzas, turkeys, entrees, snacks, desserts, ice cream, potato products, hand-held dough-based products and seafood for retail and deli customers. Frozen food major brands include Healthy Choice, Golden Cuisine, Banquet, Marie Callender's, Butterball, Kid Cuisine, MaMa Rosa's, Rosarita, Morton, Patio, La Choy, Artel and Wolfgang Puck.

Refrigerated products.   The company makes hot dogs, bacon, ham, sausages, cold cuts, turkey products, ethnic foods, kosher products, meat alternative products, egg alternatives and dessert toppings for retail and deli customers. Major brands include Armour, Butterball, Cook's, Decker, Eckrich, Healthy Choice, Louis Kemp, Ready Crisp, Hebrew National, Brown 'N Serve, Lightlife, National Deli, Parkay, Blue Bonnet, Fleischmann's, Egg Beaters and Reddi-wip.

ConAgra is also a leader in the food services and food ingredients segments.

ConAgra has grown through a long series of acquisitions. Recent acquisitions include Beatrice Company in 1990, Golden Valley Microwave Foods in 1992 and International Home Foods in 2001. The International Home Foods acquisition brought in a number of well-known brands, including Chef Boyardee, Gulden's, Libby's, PAM, and Louis Kemp.

Founded n 1919, ConAgra has 63,000 employees and a market capitalization of $14 billion.

Dividend Yield   ☆ ☆ ☆
4.0 percent (2004)

Dividend Growth (past five years)   ☆ ☆
48 percent

Consistency   ☆ ☆ ☆ ☆
Increased dividends more than 15 consecutive years.

Financial Strength   ☆ ☆
Increased earnings per share three of the past five years.
Increased revenues three of the past five years.

Financial Summary
Fiscal year ended: May 31

	1999	2000	2001	2002	2003	2004	5-Year Growth (%)
Dividends/share ($)	.69	.79	.86	.93	.98	1.02	48
Earnings/share ($)	1.48	1.67	1.33	1.47	1.58	1.50	1
Revenue ($billions)	24.6	25.4	27.2	27.6	19.8	14.5	—
Dividend yield (%)	2.4	3.5	4.1	4.1	4.1	4.0	—

5-year stock growth (mid-1999 to mid-2004): 4 percent ($25 to $26)

Sara Lee Corp.

Three First National Plaza
Chicago, IL   60602
312-726-2600

NYSE: SLE
www.saralee.com

Chairman, CEO, and President: C. Steven McMillan

Current Yield	3.4%	
Back-to-the-Future Yield	5-year 3.8%	10-year 6.6%

Rating

Dividend Yield	☆ ☆
Dividend Growth	☆ ☆
Consistency	☆ ☆ ☆ ☆
Financial Strength	☆ ☆ ☆
Total	11 points

SARA LEE HAS SPREAD ITS FARE FAR AND WIDE. IT HAS OPERATIONS IN 55 countries, and it markets its products in nearly 200 nations on every corner of the globe. Its foreign sales account for about 42 percent of its annual revenue.

But Sara Lee is a lot more than cheesecake. It offers a broad line of consumer goods in three different categories, including:

Foods and beverages. Sara Lee's leading brands include Ball Park franks and sausages, Bryan hot dogs and other meats, Earth Grain bread, Hillshire meats, Jimmy Dean sausage, Sara Lee baked goods, and Superior coffee.

Apparel. Sara Lee is a leader in the intimate apparel sector. Its leading brands include Hanes, Playtex, Wonderbra, Champion, and Bali..

Household products. The company makes Kiwi shoe polish, Sanex bath and body care products, and Ambi Pur air freshing products.

The Chicago operation has about 146,000 employees and a market capitalization of about $18 billion.

Dividend Yield ☆ ☆
3.4 percent (2004)

Dividend Growth (past five years) ☆ ☆
53 percent

Consistency ☆ ☆ ☆ ☆
Increased dividends 10 consecutive years.

Financial Strength ☆ ☆ ☆
Increased earnings per share four of the past five years.
Increased revenues four of the past five years.

Financial Summary
Fiscal year ended: June 30

	1999	2000	2001	2002	2003	2004	5-Year Growth (%)
Dividends/share ($)	.49	.53	.57	.60	.62	.75	53
Earnings/share ($)	1.21	1.27	1.43	1.42	1.49	1.52	26
Revenue ($billions)	20.0	16.4	16.6	17.6	18.3	19.6	—
Dividend yield (%)	1.9	2.6	2.7	2.8	3.1	3.4	—

5-year stock growth (mid-1999 to mid-2004): 2 percent ($21.50 to $22)

TCF Financial

200 Lake Street East
Wayzata, MN 55391
612-661-6500

NYSE: TCB
www.tcfexpress.com

Chairman and CEO: William A. Cooper
President: Lynn A. Nagorske

Current Yield	2.4%	
Back-to-the-Future Yield	5-year 4.5%	10-year 15.5%

Rating

Dividend Yield	
Dividend Growth	☆ ☆ ☆ ☆
Consistency	☆ ☆ ☆ ☆
Financial Strength	☆ ☆ ☆
Total	11 points

TCF FINANCIAL HAS MANAGED TO KEEP ITS BANKING BUSINESS GROWING BY offering customers "totally free checking." Formerly known as Twin Cities Federal, the Wayzata, Minnesota institution lures customers in with the free checking service in hopes of engaging them in some other financial services once they're on the books.

The system has worked well for TCF, which has seen its assets double in the past 10 years despite its preference for growing from within rather than through acquisitions.

The company has 411 banking offices in Minnesota, Illinois, Michigan, Wisconsin, Colorado and Indiana. It also operates subsidiaries involved in leasing and equipment finance, mortgage banking, brokerage, and investments and insurance sales.

TCF emphasizes return on average assets, return on average equity, and earnings per share growth. Local geographic managers are responsible for local business decisions, business development initiatives, customer relations, and community involvement. Managers are given incentives to achieve those goals.

TCF had its initial stock offering in 1986. It has about 8,200 employees and a market capitalization of $4 billion.

Dividend Yield
2.4 percent (2004)

Dividend Growth (past five years)   ☆ ☆ ☆ ☆
113 percent

Consistency   ☆ ☆ ☆ ☆
Increased dividends 12 consecutive years.

Financial Strength   ☆ ☆ ☆
Increased earnings per share four of the past five years.
Increased assets four of the past five years.

Financial Summary
Fiscal year ended: Dec. 31

	1998	1999	2000	2001	2002	2003	5-Year Growth (%)
Dividends/share ($)	.61	.73	.83	1.00	1.15	1.30	113
Earnings/share ($)	1.76	2.00	2.35	2.70	3.15	3.05	73
Assets ($billions)	10.2	10.7	11.2	11.4	12.2	11.3	11
Dividend yield (%)	2.1	2.7	2.8	2.4	2.4	2.9	—

5-year stock growth (mid-1999 to mid-2004): 107 percent ($15 to $31)

Johnson & Johnson

32

One Johnson & Johnson Plaza
New Brunswick, NJ 08933
732-524-2454

NYSE: JNJ
www.jnj.com

Chairman and CEO: William Weldon

Current Yield	2.0%	
Back-to-the-Future Yield	5-year 2.2%	10-year 8.8%

Rating

Dividend Yield	
Dividend Growth	☆ ☆ ☆
Consistency	☆ ☆ ☆ ☆
Financial Strength	☆ ☆ ☆ ☆
Total	11 points

FROM BAND-AIDS AND BABY OIL TO TYLENOL AND MYLANTA, JOHNSON & Johnson has made its mark by easing the pain of millions of consumers around the world. The New Brunswick, New Jersey operation has subsidiaries in 57 foreign countries, with sales in about 175 countries. International sales make up about 40 percent of the company's total revenue.

Consumer products account for about 18 percent of the company's annual revenue. Other leading consumer products from Johnson & Johnson include Imodium A-D, Nicotrol smoking cessation products, Carefree Panty Shields, Clean & Clear Skin Care products, Monistat, Pepcid AC, Neutrogena skin and hair products, Sundown and Piz Buin sun care products, Reach toothbrushes, Act Floride Rinse, and Stayfree and Sure & Natural sanitary protection products.

In addition to its consumer products, the company has two other key divisions:

Pharmaceuticals (47 percent of total revenue). The company turns out a wide range of pharmaceuticals, including contraceptives, anti-fungal ointments, central nervous system medications, allergy and asthma medications, gastrointestinal treatments and skin care formulas.

Medical Devices and Diagnostics (35 percent). Johnson & Johnson produces a number of products for doctors and medical professionals, such as sutures, mechanical wound closure products, endoscopic products, dental products, diagnostic products, medical equipment and devices, ophthalmic products, surgical instruments and medical supplies used by physicians, dentists, therapists, hospitals and clinics. It is leading maker of contact lenses in the world.

Founded in 1887, Johnson & Johnson has about 11,000 employees and a market capitalization of about $175 billion.

Dividend Yield
2.0 percent (2004)

Dividend Growth (past five years) ☆ ☆ ☆
90 percent

Consistency ☆ ☆ ☆ ☆
Increased dividends 42 consecutive years.

Financial Strength ☆ ☆ ☆ ☆
Increased earnings by double digits 19 consecutive years.
Increased revenues 71 consecutive years.

Financial Summary
Fiscal year ended: Dec. 31

	1998	1999	2000	2001	2002	2003	5-Year Growth (%)
Dividends/share ($)	.49	.55	.62	.70	.80	.93	90
Earnings/share ($)	1.34	1.49	1.70	1.91	2.23	2.70	101
Revenue ($billions)	23.7	27.5	29.1	33.0	36.3	41.8	76
Dividend yield (%)	1.3	1.2	1.4	1.3	1.4	1.8	—

5-year stock growth (mid-1999 to mid-2004): 12 percent ($51 to $57)

Liberty Property Trust

33

65 Valley Stream Parkway, Suite 100
Malvern, PA 19355
610-648-1700

NYSE: LRY
www.libertyproperty.com

Chairman, president and CEO: William P. Hankowsky

Current Yield	6.1%	
Back-to-the-Future Yield	5-year 10.5%	10-year 12.9%

Rating

Dividend Yield	☆ ☆ ☆ ☆
Dividend Growth	☆
Consistency	☆ ☆ ☆
Financial Strength	☆ ☆
Total	10 points

LIBERTY PROPERTY TRUST OWNS AND OPERATES MORE THAN 670 INDUSTRIAL and office building covering about 54 million square feet. The Pennsylvania-based real estate investment trust (REIT) also has about 15 properties under development and owns about 1,100 acres of land currently zoned for commercial use.

Liberty is also involved in five joint ventures with interests in 30 properties and 53 acres of undeveloped land.

The company provides leasing, property management, development, acquisition and other tenant-related services for its properties.

Its industrial properties consist of a variety of warehouse, distribution, service, assembly, light manufacturing and research and development facilities. Its office properties are multi-story and single-story office buildings located principally in suburban mixed-use developments or office parks.

Office properties account for about 55 percent of its rent base and industrial properties make up the other 45 percent.

Liberty has properties in several primary areas, including the Delaware Valley (southeastern Pennsylvania and New Jersey), which accounts for 33 percent of its rent base; the Midwest, which brings in 30 percent of rent revenues; the Mid-Atlantic, 19 percent; and Florida, 15 percent. About three percent of its rent is generated in other areas, including the County of Kent in the United Kingdom.

Founded in 1972 as Rouse and Associates, the company changed its name to Liberty Property Trust in 1994. That's when it was reorganized as a REIT and made its initial public stock offering. Liberty has about 400 employees and a stock market capitalization of about $3.3 billion.

Dividend Yield   ☆ ☆ ☆ ☆
6.3 percent (2004)

Dividend Growth (past five years)   ☆
41 percent

Consistency   ☆ ☆ ☆
Increased dividends eight consecutive years.

Financial Strength   ☆ ☆
Increased earnings three of the past five years.
Increased revenues five of the past five years.

Financial Summary
Fiscal year ended: Dec. 31

	1998	1999	2000	2001	2002	2003	5-Year Growth (%)
Dividends/share ($)	1.71	1.87	2.13	2.30	2.38	2.41	41
Earnings/share ($)	1.59	1.95	2.17	2.15	1.97	2.05	29
Revenue ($millions)	388	461	523	573	593	625	61
Dividend yield (%)	6.8	8.0	8.3	8.1	7.6	7.1	—

5-year stock growth (mid-1999 to mid-2004): 67 percent ($24 to $40)

Buckeye Partners, L.P.

34

P.O. Box 368
Emmaus, PA 18049
800-422-2825

NYSE: BPL
www.buckeye.com

President and CEO: William H. Shea

Current Yield	6.7%	
Back-to-the-Future Yield	5-year 9.5%	10-year 14.3%

Rating

Dividend Yield	☆ ☆ ☆ ☆
Dividend Growth	☆
Consistency	☆ ☆ ☆
Financial Strength	☆ ☆
Total	**10 points**

BUCKEYE PARTNERS PUMPS REFINED PETROLEUM THROUGH 3,800 MILES OF pipeline in a 10-state area in the Midwest and Northeast. It also operates approximately 1,200 miles of pipeline under agreement with major oil and chemical companies, and provides bulk storage services at terminals in Illinois, Indiana, Michigan, New York, Ohio and Pennsylvania.

Buckeye, which is a publicly-traded limited partnership, is one of the nation's largest independent pipeline common carriers of refined petroleum products.

Through its extensive pipeline network, Buckeye provides refiners, wholesalers, marketers and commercial end-users with a variety of petroleum products, such as gasoline, jet fuel, diesel fuel, heating oil, and kerosene. It also transports other refined products, such as propane and butane, refinery feed stocks and blending components.

Gasoline is the company's largest volume product, accounting for about 51 percent of total volume. Jet fuel accounts for about 22 percent, and distillates make up 25 percent.

Buckeye was founded in 1886 as part of the Standard Oil Company to gather crude oil in northwestern Ohio. In 1911, when Standard Oil was dissolved, Buckeye became a publicly owned, independent company. In 1986, Buckeye was reorganized into a master limited partnership. The company has a market capitalization of about $1.1 billion.

Dividend Yield   ☆ ☆ ☆ ☆
6.7 percent (2004)

Dividend Growth (past five years)   ☆
21 percent

Consistency   ☆ ☆ ☆
Increased dividends eight consecutive years.

Financial Strength   ☆ ☆
Increased earnings per share three of the past five years.
Increased revenues four of the past five years.

Financial Summary
Fiscal year ended: Dec. 31

	1998	1999	2000	2001	2002	2003	5-Year Growth (%)
Dividends/share ($)	2.10	2.18	2.40	2.45	2.50	2.54	21
Earnings/share ($)	2.05	2.41	2.38	2.56	2.65	2.64	29
Revenue ($millions)	185	306	209	232	247	272	61
Dividend yield (%)	7.4	8.0	8.7	7.1	6.8	6.5	—

5-year stock growth (mid-1999 to mid-2004): 46 percent ($28 to $41)

Pinnacle West Capital Corp.

35

400 E. Van Buren St., Suite 700
P.O. Box 52132
Phoenix, AZ 85072
602-379-2568

NYSE: PNW
www.pinnaclewest.com

Chairman and CEO: William J. Post
President: Jack E. Davis

Current Yield	4.3%	
Back-to-the-Future Yield	5-year 4.8%	10-year 9.2%

Rating

Dividend Yield	☆ ☆ ☆
Dividend Growth	☆
Consistency	☆ ☆ ☆ ☆
Financial Strength	☆ ☆
Total	**10 points**

THE PARENT COMPANY OF ARIZONA PUBLIC SERVICE, PINNACLE WEST supplies electricity to nearly one million Arizona residents.

The service area of the Phoenix-based utility encompasses nearly the entire state with the exception the Tucson metropolitan area and about half of the Phoenix metropolitan area.

The company purchases about 54 percent of its energy from outside sources. Pinnacle generates the rest itself—20 percent from coal, 11 percent from gas and related sources, and 15 percent from nuclear power. Pinnacle is a co-owner of the Palo Verde Nuclear Generating Station.

Residential customers account for about half of the company's annual revenue, while commercial and industrial customers make up the other half.

Although Arizona Public Service contributes the vast majority of Pinnacle's revenue, the company also operates three other key subsidiaries. SunCor Development Company is a developer of residential, commercial and industrial real estate; APS Energy Services is a retail energy provider the Western U.S.; and Pinnacle West Energy owns and operates electricity generating plants.

Pinnacle was incorporated in 1985 as a holding company for Arizona Public Service, which was founded more than a century ago. The company has about 7,200 employees and a market capitalization of about $4 billion.

Dividend Yield   ☆ ☆ ☆
4.3 percent (2004)

Dividend Growth (past five years)   ☆
41 percent

Consistency   ☆ ☆ ☆ ☆
Increased dividends 10 consecutive years.

Financial Strength   ☆ ☆
Increased earnings per share three of the past five years.
Increased revenues four of the past five years.

Financial Summary
Fiscal year ended: Dec. 31

	1998	1999	2000	2001	2002	2003	5-Year Growth (%)
Dividends/share ($)	1.23	1.33	1.43	1.53	1.63	1.73	41
Earnings/share ($)	2.85	3.18	3.35	3.68	2.53	2.52	—
Revenue ($billions)	2.13	2.42	3.69	4.55	2.64	2.82	32
Dividend yield (%)	2.8	3.5	3.8	3.5	4.5	4.9	—

5-year stock growth (mid-1999 to mid-2004): 8 percent ($38 to $41)

Black Hills Corp. **36**

P.O. Box 1400
Rapid City, SD 57709
605-721-1700

NYSE: BKH
www.blackhillscorp.com

Chairman: Daniel P. Landguth
President and CEO: David R. Emery

Current Yield	4.4%	
Back-to-the-Future Yield	5-year 5.2%	10-year 9.0%

Rating

Dividend Yield	☆ ☆ ☆
Dividend Growth	☆
Consistency	☆ ☆ ☆ ☆
Financial Strength	☆ ☆
Total	10 points

BLACK HILLS CORP. IS AN ELECTRIC UTILITY COMPANY THAT SERVES ABOUT 61,000 customers in South Dakota, Wyoming and Montana.

The company also produces and sells wholesale energy through a group of generating plants, and it produces coal, natural gas and crude oil primarily in the Rocky Mountain region.

Residential customers account for about 22 percent of its electric revenue, commercial customers account for 28 percent, industrial customers make up 11 percent, and wholesale sales and other sources account for 39 percent.

Coal accounts for about 80 percent of its power generation, while oil and gas make up 10 percent. It purchases the other 10 percent from other sources.

In addition to its energy services, the Rapid City, South Dakota utility also offers broadband telecommunications services, including local and long distance telephone services, cable TV, cable modem Internet, and high speed data and video services to about 27,000 residential and business customers located in Rapid City area.

Founded in 1941, Black Hills has about 870 employees and a market capitalization of about $900 million.

Dividend Yield
4.4 percent (2004)

Dividend Growth (past five years)
20 percent

Consistency
Increased dividends more than 15 consecutive years.

Financial Strength
Increased earnings per share three of the past five years.
Increased revenues four of the past five years.

Financial Summary
Fiscal year ended: Dec. 31

	1998	1999	2000	2001	2002	2003	5-Year Growth (%)
Dividends/share ($)	1.00	1.04	1.08	1.12	1.16	1.20	20
Earnings/share ($)	1.60	1.70	2.37	3.42	2.33	1.84	15
Revenue ($billions)	.540	.547	.741	.738	.908	1.25	131
Dividend yield (%)	4.2	4.5	4.2	2.9	4.0	4.1	—

5-year stock growth (mid-1999 to mid-2004): 23 percent ($22 to $27)

Piedmont Natural Gas Co.

37

1915 Rexford Road
P.O. Box 33068
Charlotte, NC 28233
704-364-3120

NYSE: PNY
www.piedmontng.com

Chairman, president and CEO: Thomas E. Skains

Current Yield	4.1%	
Back-to-the-Future Yield	5-year 5.2%	10-year 8.2%

Rating

Dividend Yield	☆ ☆ ☆
Dividend Growth	☆
Consistency	☆ ☆ ☆ ☆
Financial Strength	☆ ☆
Total	10 points

PIEDMONT NATURAL GAS DISTRIBUTES GAS TO NEARLY A MILLION residential, commercial and industrial customers in North Carolina, South Carolina and Tennessee.

In addition to its natural gas sales, the Charlotte, North Carolina, operation also owns some subsidiaries involved in related areas of the natural gas industry, including retail marketing of propane, interstate natural gas storage, intrastate natural gas transportation, and sales of residential and commercial gas appliances.

The company's biggest market area outside of Charlotte is Nashville, Tennessee. Piedmont also has customers throughout North Carolina and in the three South Carolina cities of Anderson, Greenville and Spartanburg.

Piedmont's primary revenue segments include residential gas sales (43 percent of total revenue), commercial (25 percent), industrial (9 percent), and other related areas (23 percent).

Founded in 1950, Piedmont has about 2,155 employees and a market capitalization of about $1.8 billion.

Dividend Yield ☆ ☆ ☆
4.1 percent (2004)

Dividend Growth (past five years) ☆
29 percent

Consistency ☆ ☆ ☆ ☆
Increased dividends more than 15 consecutive years.

Financial Strength ☆ ☆
Increased earnings per share three of the past five years.
Increased revenues three of the past five years.

Financial Summary
Fiscal year ended: Oct. 31

	1998	1999	2000	2001	2002	2003	5-Year Growth (%)
Dividends/share ($)	1.28	1.36	1.44	1.52	1.60	1.65	29
Earnings/share ($)	1.96	1.86	2.01	2.02	1.89	2.22	13
Revenue ($billions)	.77	.67	.83	1.11	.83	1.22	59
Dividend yield (%)	4.0	4.1	5.0	4.5	4.8	4.4	—

5-year stock growth (late-1999 to late-2004): 44 percent ($16 to $23)

National Fuel Gas Co.

6363 Main St.
Williamsville, NY 14221
716-857-7000

NYSE: NFG
www.nationalfuelgas.com

Chairman, CEO, and President: Philip C. Ackerman

Current Yield	4.5%	
Back-to-the-Future Yield	5-year 4.8%	10-year 7.1%

Rating

Dividend Yield	☆ ☆ ☆
Dividend Growth	
Consistency	☆ ☆ ☆ ☆
Financial Strength	☆ ☆ ☆
Total	**10 points**

NATIONAL FUEL GAS WEARS SEVERAL HATS IN THE NATURAL GAS BUSINESS IN New York and Pennsylvania.

The Williamsville, New York operation breaks its business into several key segments:

Gas utility (13 percent of earnings). The company sells and delivers natural gas to about 733,000 customers in western New York and northwestern Pennsylvania.

Pipeline and storage (25 percent). The firm owns and operates gas pipelines in Pennsylvania and New York in the Buffalo area near the Canadian border. It transmits gas to customers in that region through a pipeline network that encompasses nearly 3,000 miles of pipeline.

Timber harvesting and other divisions (42 percent). The company is involved in the timber industry through its subsidiaries. Seneca

Resources owns over 80,000 acres of timber property in Pennsylvania and New York and Highland Forest Resources owns and operates two sawmills in Pennsylvania. Seneca Resources is also involved in the exploration and development of natural gas in the Gulf of Mexico.

Founded in 1902, National Fuel Gas has about 3,000 employees and a market capitalization of about $2 billion.

Dividend Yield ☆ ☆ ☆
4.5 percent (2004)

Dividend Growth (past five years)
18 percent

Consistency ☆ ☆ ☆ ☆
Increased dividends more than 15 consecutive years.

Financial Strength ☆ ☆ ☆
Increased earnings per share four of the past five years.
Increased revenue four of the past five years.

Financial Summary
Fiscal year ended: Dec. 31

	1998	1999	2000	2001	2002	2003	5-Year Growth (%)
Dividends/share ($)	.89	.92	.95	.99	1.03	1.06	3
Earnings/share ($)	1.44	1.47	1.61	0.82	1.46	2.30	60
Revenue ($billions)	1.25	1.26	1.41	2.06	1.46	2.04	63
Dividend yield (%)	3.9	4.0	3.9	3.7	4.6	4.7	—

5-year stock growth (late-1999 to late-2004): 8 percent ($26 to $28)

WPS Resources Corp.

700 N. Adams St.
Green Bay, WI 54307
800-236-1551

NYSE: WPS
www.wpsr.com

Chairman, president and CEO: Larry L. Weyers

Current Yield	4.7 %	
Back-to-the-Future Yield	5-year 7.2%	10-year 8.7%

Rating

Dividend Yield	☆ ☆ ☆
Dividend Growth	
Consistency	☆ ☆ ☆ ☆
Financial Strength	☆ ☆ ☆
Total	10 points

WPS RESOURCES IS THE PARENT COMPANY OF WISCONSIN PUBLIC SERVICE, an electric and natural gas utility that serves customers in Wisconsin and Upper Michigan.

In all, the Green Bay, Wisconsin utility serves 414,295 retail electric customers and 300,859 natural gas retail customers

The firm also operates three other subsidiaries:

Upper Peninsula Power Company. An electric utility, the company serves about 50,000 customers in two-thirds of Michigan's Upper Peninsula.

WPS Energy Services. This diversified, non-regulated energy firm provides natural gas and electricity to parts of Illinois, Maine, Michigan, Ohio and Wisconsin.

WPS Power Development. The operation owns electric generation facilities in Wisconsin, Maine, Pennsylvania, New York and New

Brunswick, Canada. It also holds a 23 percent interest in a synthetic fuel processing facility located in Kentucky and steam production facilities located in Arkansas and Oregon.

Founded in 1883, WPS has about 3,080 employees and a market capitalization of about $1.7 billion.

Dividend Yield   ☆ ☆ ☆
4.7 percent (2004)

Dividend Growth (past five years)
10 percent

Consistency   ☆ ☆ ☆ ☆
Has increased dividends more than 15 consecutive years.

Financial Strength   ☆ ☆ ☆
Increased earnings per four of the past five years.
Increased revenues four of the past five years.

Financial Summary
Fiscal year ended: Dec. 31

	1998	1999	2000	2001	2002	2003	5-Year Growth (%)
Dividends/share ($)	1.96	2.00	2.04	2.08	2.12	2.16	10
Earnings/share ($)	1.76	2.24	2.43	2.74	2.74	2.76	57
Revenue ($billions)	1.06	1.10	1.95	2.68	2.67	4.32	308
Dividend yield (%)	5.9	6.7	6.9	6.1	5.5	5.3	—

5-year stock growth (mid-1999 to mid-2004): 62 percent ($29 to $47)

Washington Federal, Inc.

40

425 Pike St.
Seattle, WA 98101
206-624-7930

Nasdaq: WFSL
www.washingtonfederal.com

Chairman: Guy C. Pinkerton
CEO, and President: Roy M. Whitehead

Current Yield	3.6%	
Back-to-the-Future Yield	5-year 5.4%	10-year 8.3%

Rating

Dividend Yield	☆ ☆
Dividend Growth	☆
Consistency	☆ ☆ ☆ ☆
Financial Strength	☆ ☆ ☆
Total	**10 points**

WASHINGTON FEDERAL TAKES A UNIQUE APPROACH TO ITS BANKING business. The Seattle institution raises investment money primarily by attracting savings deposits from the general public and invests most of it in loans secured by first mortgages on single-family homes.

The firm has 114 branches throughout Washington, Oregon, Idaho, Arizona, Utah, Nevada and Texas. It also has a loan production office in Colorado. It is also involved in real estate development and the insurance brokerage business.

For its banking customers, the company offers the standard consumer banking services, such as checking, savings, and consumer loans.

Washington Federal traces its roots to 1917, when Ballard Savings and Loan Association was established in a fishing and lumber community north of Seattle.

In 1982 the association converted from a federal mutual to a federal stock association, and in 1995 formed a holding company, Washington Federal, Inc.

Washington Federal has grown both internally and through acquisitions. In all it has acquired 11 other banks, although the last acquisition was in 1996.

The company has about 760 employees and a market capitalization of about $2 billion.

Dividend Yield   ☆ ☆
3.6 percent (2004)

Dividend Growth (past five years)   ☆
39 percent

Consistency   ☆ ☆ ☆ ☆
Increased dividends more than 10 consecutive years.

Financial Strength   ☆ ☆ ☆
Increased earnings per share four of the past five years.
Increased assets past five consecutive years.

Financial Summary
Fiscal year ended: Dec. 31

	1998	1999	2000	2001	2002	2003	5-Year Growth (%)
Dividends/share ($)	.56	.61	.67	.71	.74	.78	3
Earnings/share ($)	1.32	1.40	1.37	1.47	1.86	1.88	42
Assets ($billions)	5.6	6.2	6.7	7.0	7.4	7.5	34
Dividend yield (%)	3.3	3.9	5.2	3.9	3.7	3.8	—

5-year stock growth (late-1999 to late-2004): 56 percent ($16 to $25)

Wilmington Trust Corp.

41

Rodney Square North
1100 N. Market St.
Wilmington, DE 19890
302-651-1000

NYSE: WL
www.wilmingtontrust.com

Chairman and CEO: Ted T. Cecala

Current Yield	3.3%	
Back-to-the-Future Yield	5-year 4.0%	10-year 8.7%

Rating

Dividend Yield	☆ ☆
Dividend Growth	☆
Consistency	☆ ☆ ☆ ☆
Financial Strength	☆ ☆ ☆
Total	10 points

WILMINGTON TRUST IS A CENTURY OLD BANKING ORGANIZATION THAT caters to consumer and commercial customers in the mid-Atlanta region. In addition to the typical banking services, the bank also focuses on wealth advisory and corporate client services.

The company was founded in 1901 and paid its first dividend in 1908. It has paid dividends every year since.

Wilmington Trust is the largest bank in Delaware, with 45 branch offices in the state. It offers the usual consumer banking services, such as checking, savings, consumer and business loans, mortgages, certificates of deposit, and other investment products. Although it is a relatively small regional operation with assets of under $9 billion, Wilmington Trust boasts clients on six continents and in all 50 states.

Its loan portfolio consists of commercial loans (36 percent), installment loans (27 percent), commercial mortgages (17 percent), residential mortgages (10 percent), and real estate construction (10 percent).

In addition to its concentration of branch offices in Delaware, the firm also operates offices in Pennsylvania, Maryland, Florida, and California. It also some investment advisory firms in the New England area.

Wilmington's wealth advisory business serves clients throughout the U.S. and about 35 foreign countries. The corporate client business provides specialty trust services for national and multinational institutions. The regional banking business targets commercial and consumer clients throughout the Delaware Valley region.

The company has 2,300 employees and a market capitalization of about $2.3 billion.

Dividend Yield ☆ ☆
3.3 percent (2004)

Dividend Growth (past five years) ☆
39 percent

Consistency ☆ ☆ ☆ ☆
Increased dividends more than 15 consecutive years.

Financial Strength ☆ ☆ ☆
Increased earnings per share four of the past five years.
Increased assets for more than 10 consecutive years.

Financial Summary
Fiscal year ended: Dec. 31

	1998	1999	2000	2001	2002	2003	5-Year Growth (%)
Dividends/share ($)	0.77	0.83	0.89	0.95	1.01	1.07	3
Earnings/share ($)	1.67	1.61	1.85	1.90	2.01	2.02	21
Assets ($billions)	6.3	7.2	7.3	7.5	8.1	8.5	35
Dividend yield (%)	2.6	3.0	3.6	3.1	3.2	3.5	—

5-year stock growth (late-1999 to late-2004): 21 percent ($28 to $34)

Abbott Laboratories

42

One Abbott Park Road
North Chicago, IL 60064
847-937-6100

NYSE: ABT
www.abbott.com

Chairman and CEO: Miles D. White

Current Yield	2.4%	
Back-to-the-Future Yield	5-year 2.5%	10-year 6.8%

Rating

Dividend Yield	
Dividend Growth	☆ ☆
Consistency	☆ ☆ ☆ ☆
Financial Strength	☆ ☆ ☆ ☆
Total	10 points

FOR MORE THAN A CENTURY, ABBOTT LABORATORIES HAS BEEN DEVELOPING drugs and diagnostic testing products for doctors and hospitals the world over. The Chicago-based operation was founded in 1888. It is one of the world's leading makers of blood screening equipment, and was the first company to introduce an AIDS antibody test.

Abbott is also among the leaders in tests for hepatitis, sexually transmitted diseases, cancer, thyroid function, pregnancy, illicit drugs and drug monitoring. With more than 30 consecutive years of increased sales and earnings, Abbott has been one of the nation's most consistent companies.

Its leading consumer products include Murine, Similac, Isomil, Tricor, Formax, and Humira.

The company breaks its operations into three key segments, including:

Pharmaceuticals and nutritional products (38 percent of total revenue). The firm produces a broad line of adult and pediatric pharmaceuticals, including treatments for epilepsy, migraine, and bipolar disorder, benign prostatic hyperplasia, arthritis, hypertension, and HIV infection.

Household and Diagnostic products (32 percent of revenue). Abbott's leading diagnostic products include testing products for hepatitis, HIV antibodies and antigens, and other infectious diseases. It also makes clinical testing products for cancer, fertility, pregnancy, and drug abuse.

International (30 percent). Abbott offers a broad line of hospital, pharmaceutical and pediatric nutritional products that are made and marketed outside the U.S. It has sales or operations in more than 130 countries.

The company has more than 130 research, manufacturing and distribution facilities worldwide. Abbott Laboratories was founded in 1888 by Dr. Wallace C. Abbott, who began the business as a sideline venture in his small Chicago apartment, making pills from the alkaloid of plants.

Abbott has about 72,000 employees and a market capitalization of about $65 billion.

Dividend Yield
2.4 percent (2004)

Dividend Growth (past five years) ☆ ☆
61 percent

Consistency ☆ ☆ ☆ ☆
Increased dividends more than 15 consecutive years.

Financial Strength ☆ ☆ ☆ ☆
Increased earnings per share more 30 consecutive years.
Increased revenue more than 30 consecutive years.

Financial Summary
Fiscal year ended: Dec. 31

	1998	1999	2000	2001	2002	2003	5-Year Growth (%)
Dividends/share ($)	0.60	0.66	0.74	0.82	0.92	0.97	6
Earnings/share ($)	1.51	1.66	1.78	1.88	2.06	2.21	71
Revenue ($billions)	12.8	13.2	13.7	16.3	17.7	19.7	37
Dividend yield (%)	1.5	1.5	1.8	1.6	2.0	2.3	—

5-year stock growth (mid-1999 to mid-2004): -9 percent ($45 to $41)

Cincinnati Financial Corp.

43

6200 S. Gilmore Road
Fairfield, OH 45014
513-870-2000

NASDAQ: CINF
www.cinfin.com

Chairman and CEO: J. J. Schiff, Jr.

Current Yield	2.6%	
Back-to-the-Future Yield	5-year 2.9%	10-year 6.8%

Rating

Dividend Yield	☆
Dividend Growth	☆ ☆
Consistency	☆ ☆ ☆ ☆
Financial Strength	☆ ☆ ☆
Total	10 points

CINCINNATI FINANCIAL OFFERS A BROAD RANGE OF INSURANCE PRODUCTS, although its bread and butter is property and casualty.

The company operates through six primary subsidiaries. The Cincinnati Insurance Company is its lead property and casualty subsidiary, although The Cincinnati Casualty Company and the Cincinnati Indemnity Company also offer business, homeowner, auto and personal liability insurance.

The Cincinnati Life Insurance Company markets life and disability income insurance and annuities. The CFC Investment Company oversees the company's insurance subsidiaries and independent agent representatives through commercial leasing and financing activities. CinFin Capital Management Company provides asset management services to institutions, corporations and individuals.

The company markets insurance policies through a network of 1,100 employees in field locations and nearly 1,000 independent agents.

The company sells property and casualty insurance in 31 states. About 72 percent of its property and casualty sales are commercial lines while the other 28 percent are personal lines.

Founded in 1968, Cincinnati Financial has about 3,650 employees and a market capitalization of about $7.2 billion.

Dividend Yield ☆
2.6 percent (2004)

Dividend Growth (past five years) ☆ ☆
64 percent

Consistency ☆ ☆ ☆ ☆
Increased dividends more than 15 consecutive years.

Financial Strength
Increased earnings per share four of the past five years.
Increased assets five of the past five years.

Financial Summary
Fiscal year ended: Dec. 31

	1998	1999	2000	2001	2002	2003	5-Year Growth (%)
Dividends/share ($)	.58	.65	.72	.80	.85	.95	64
Earnings/share ($)	1.34	1.45	.70	1.13	1.75	2.27	69
Assets ($billions)	11.1	11.4	13.3	14.0	14.1	15.5	40
Dividend yield (%)	1.6	1.9	2.1	2.2	2.2	2.6	—

5-year stock growth (mid-1999 to mid-2004): 11 percent ($36 to $40)

General Electric Company

44

3135 Easton Turnpike
Fairfield, CT 06431
203-373-2211

NYSE: GE
www.ge.com

Chairman and CEO: Jeffrey Immett

Current Yield	2.4%	
Back-to-the-Future Yield	5-year 1.9%	10-year 9.5%

Rating

Dividend Yield	
Dividend Growth	☆ ☆ ☆
Consistency	☆ ☆ ☆ ☆
Financial Strength	☆ ☆ ☆
Total	10 points

FROM LIGHTS AND LAMPS TO LOCOMOTIVES AND JET ENGINES, FROM consumer finance to refrigerators and freezers, from TV networks to power turbines, General Electric is one of the world's largest and most diversified industrial conglomerates.

The Fairfield, Connecticut operation is involved in a wide range of businesses, including:

Aircraft Engines. GE manufactures engines and replacement parts for commercial aircraft, executive and commuter aircraft, and military fighters, bombers, tankers and helicopters.

Commercial Finance. GE offers loans, financing and operating leases for equipment manufacturers and distributors, residential real estate, vehicles, aircraft, and equipment used in construction, manufacturing, data processing and office applications, electronics and telecommunications, and healthcare.

Consumer Finance. The company offers private-label credit card loans, personal loans, time sales and revolving credit, residential mortgage financing and inventory financing for retail merchants, and auto leasing and inventory financing.

Consumer Products. GE manufactures major home appliances such as refrigerators, freezers, electric and gas ranges, cook tops, dishwashers, clothes washers and dryers, microwave ovens, room air conditioners and residential water systems. It also makes a wide variety of lamps, lighting fixtures and wiring devices.

Industrial Products and Systems. GE makes electrical distribution and control equipment (including power delivery and control products such as transformers, meters, and capacitors); measurement and sensing equipment, security equipment and systems, transportation systems (including diesel and electric locomotives, transit propulsion equipment, motorized wheels for off-highway vehicles, and railway signaling communications systems); electric motors and related products; and a broad range of electrical and electronic industrial automation products.

Materials. GE makes engineered plastics used in applications such as automobiles and housings for computers and other business equipment; resins, silicones, industrial diamonds, quartz products, and laminates.

NBC. GE owns NBC, CNBC, and MSNBC as well as a number of affiliate TV stations in major metro markets throughout the U.S.

Power Systems. GE manufactures power plant products, including gas turbines, steam turbines, and generators.

Foreign sales account for about half of the company's total revenue.

GE traces its roots to the Edison Electric Company, founded in 1878 by the great Thomas Edison. GE has about 305,000 employees and a market capitalization of about $330 billion.

Dividend Yield
2.4 percent (2004)

Dividend Growth (past five years)   ☆ ☆ ☆
83 percent

Consistency   ☆ ☆ ☆ ☆
Increased dividends more 28 consecutive years.

Financial Strength   ☆ ☆ ☆
Increased earnings per share five of the past five years.
Increased revenues four of the past five years.

Financial Summary
Fiscal year ended: Dec. 31

	1998	1999	2000	2001	2002	2003	5-Year Growth (%)
Dividends/share ($)	.42	.49	.57	.64	.72	.77	83
Earnings/share ($)	.93	1.07	1.28	1.36	1.41	1.49	75
Revenue ($billions)	100	112	130	126	132	134	34
Dividend yield (%)	1.5	1.3	1.1	1.5	2.3	2.7	—

5-year stock growth (mid-1999 to mid-2004): -15 percent ($40 to $34)

Comerica, Inc.

45

Comerica Tower at Detroit Center
Detroit, MI 48226
313-222-3300

NYSE: CMA
www.comerica.com

Chairman and CEO: Ralph Babb, Jr.

Current Yield	3.4%	
Back-to-the-Future Yield	5-year 3.5%	10-year 5.5%

Rating

Dividend Yield	☆ ☆
Dividend Growth	☆ ☆
Consistency	☆ ☆ ☆ ☆
Financial Strength	☆ ☆
Total	10 points

COMERICA IS THE LARGEST BANK IN MICHIGAN AND ONE OF THE 20 LARGEST banks in America. It has more than 350 branch offices and more than 500 ATMs.

Outside of Michigan, the Detroit-based institution has operations in Florida, Texas, and California.

The company breaks its operations into three key segments:

The Business Bank. This division is comprised of middle market, commercial real estate, national dealer services, global finance, large corporate, leasing, financial services group and technology and life sciences lending. It caters to medium-size businesses, multinational corporations and governmental entities by offering various products and services, including commercial loans and lines of credit, deposits, cash management, capital market products, international trade finance, letters of credit, foreign exchange management services and loan syndication services.

Small Business and Personal Financial Services. The company provides consumer lending, consumer deposit gathering and mortgage loan origination, as well as a variety of consumer products, including deposit accounts, installment loans, credit cards, student loans, home equity lines of credit and residential mortgage loans.

Wealth and Institutional Management. Comerica offers private banking, personal and institutional trust, retirement plans, and asset management. This division also includes Comerica Securities, which offers institutional, retail and discount brokerage, and investment banking services, as well as Comerica Insurance, which is a full line insurance agency.

The company's loan portfolio breaks down this way: commercial loans, 57 percent; real estate, 30 percent; consumer, 4 percent; international, 6 percent; and lease financing, 3 percent.

Founded in 1849 as Detroit Savings Fund Institute, Comerica has about 11,300 employees and a market capitalization of about $10 billion.

Dividend Yield ☆ ☆
3.4 percent (2004)

Dividend Growth (past five years) ☆ ☆
55 percent

Consistency ☆ ☆ ☆ ☆
Increased dividends more than 15 consecutive years.

Financial Strength ☆ ☆
Increased earnings per share three of the past five years.
Increased assets four of the past five years.

Financial Summary
Fiscal year ended: Dec. 31

	1998	1999	2000	2001	2002	2003	5-Year Growth (%)
Dividends/share ($)	1.28	1.44	1.56	1.72	1.88	1.98	55
Earnings/share ($)	3.72	4.14	4.63	4.61	3.40	3.75	1
Assets ($billions)	36.6	38.7	42	50.7	53.3	52.6	44
Dividend yield (%)	2.0	2.5	3.2	3.0	3.4	4.3	—

5-year stock growth (mid-1999 to mid-2004): 9 percent ($54 to $59)

Atmos Energy Corp.

46

P.O. Box 650205
Dallas, TX 75265
972-934-9227

NYSE: ATO
www.atmosenergy.com

Chairman, president and CEO: Robert W. Best

Current Yield	5.1%	
Back-to-the-Future Yield	5-year 4.6%	10-year 6.7%

Rating

Dividend Yield	☆ ☆ ☆ ☆
Dividend Growth	
Consistency	☆ ☆ ☆ ☆
Financial Strength	☆ ☆
Total	10 points

ATMOS ENERGY IS ONE OF THE NATION'S LARGEST DISTRIBUTORS OF NATURAL gas. The Dallas-based operation delivers gas to about 1.7 million residential, commercial, industrial and public-authority customers throughout much of the Southwest United States, as well as the Southern and Appalachian states.

In all, Atmos has customers in more than a thousand communities in 12 states. The company has grown primarily by acquiring other utilities. It recently acquired Mississippi Valley Gas Company, which is the Mississippi's largest natural gas utility.

Atmos Energy's utility operations account for about 87 percent of its consolidated net income.

In addition to its utility services, Atmos also markets gas supplies to industrial customers and municipalities in 18 states. As part of the service, it arranges for gas transportation and management services, manages gas storage and pipeline equipment, and constructs and leases small electric generating plants for municipalities and industrial customers.

Atmos traces its roots to 1906, although it did not take its present name until 1988. Atmos has about 2,900 employees and a market capitalization of about $1.3 billion.

Dividend Yield ☆ ☆ ☆ ☆
5.1 percent (2004)

Dividend Growth (past five years)
13 percent

Consistency ☆ ☆ ☆ ☆
Increased its dividend 20 consecutive years.

Financial Strength ☆ ☆
Increased earnings per share three of the past five years.
Increased revenue three of the past five years.

Financial Summary
Fiscal year ended: Sept. 30

	1998	1999	2000	2001	2002	2003	5-Year Growth (%)
Dividends/share ($)	1.06	1.10	1.14	1.16	1.18	1.20	13
Earnings/share ($)	1.84	0.58	1.14	1.47	1.45	1.54	—
Revenue ($billions)	.85	.69	.85	1.72	1.65	2.8	88
Dividend yield (%)	3.7	4.1	5.9	5.1	5.4	5.2	—

5-year stock growth (late-1999 to late-2004): 9 percent ($23 to $25)

National Bank of Canada

47

National Bank Tower
600 de La Gauchetiere West
Montreal, Quebec, Canada H3B 4L2
514-394-4000

TSE (Toronto): NA.TO
www.nbc.ca

President and CEO: Real Raymond

Current Yield	3.4%	
Back-to-the-Future Yield	5-year 6.2%	10-year 13.2%

Rating

Dividend Yield	☆ ☆
Dividend Growth	☆ ☆
Consistency	☆ ☆ ☆
Financial Strength	☆ ☆
Total	9 points

THE NATIONAL BANK OF CANADA HAS NEARLY 500 BRANCHES THROUGHOUT Canada, as well as offices in the U.S. and 20 other foreign countries.

The Montreal-based institution is nearly 140 years old. It is the sixth largest bank in Canada.

Its loan portfolio includes business and government loans (45 percent), residential mortgages (33 percent), repurchase agreements (8 percent), and other a variety of other types of loans (14 percent).

The bank plays an active role in the international capital markets, and is involved in securities brokerage, insurance and wealth management, and mutual fund and retirement plan management.

In 2002, the company acquired the U.S. financial services company Putnam Lovell Group. The firm offers services through offices in New York, San Francisco, Los Angeles, Toronto, and London.

Founded in 1859, the National Bank of Canada has about 16,300 employees and a market capitalization of about $7 billion (Canadian dollars).

Dividend Yield
3.4 percent (2004)

Dividend Growth (past five years)
64 percent

Consistency
Increased dividends nine consecutive years.

Financial Strength
Increased earnings per share four of the past five years.
Increased assets two of the past five years.

Financial Summary
Fiscal year ended: Oct. 31
All figures are Canadian Dollars

	1998	1999	2000	2001	2002	2003	5-Year Growth (%)
Dividends/share ($)	.66	.70	.75	.82	.93	1.08	64
Earnings/share ($)	2.05	2.27	2.52	2.87	2.86	3.33	62
Assets ($billions)	70.7	69.8	75.8	75.8	74.6	82.4	17
Dividend yield (%)	2.6	3.3	3.6	3.0	3.1	3.1	—

5-year stock growth (mid-1999 to mid-2004): 131 percent ($19 to $44 Canadian Dollars)

Health Care Property Investors, Inc. 48

3760 Kilroy Airport Way, Suite 300
Long Beach, CA 90806
562-733–5100

NYSE: HCP
www.hcpi.com

Chairman: Kenneth B. Roath
President and CEO: James Flaherty III

Current Yield	7.0%	
Back-to-the-Future Yield	5-year 12.3%	10-year 11.4%

Rating

Dividend Yield	☆ ☆ ☆ ☆
Dividend Growth	☆
Consistency	☆ ☆ ☆ ☆
Financial Strength	
Total	9 points

AS ITS NAME IMPLIES, HEALTH CARE PROPERTY INVESTORS (HCPI) OWNS real estate properties that are involved in the business of health care. That includes hospitals, nursing homes, medical office buildings, retirement and assisted living centers, and other health care facilities.

The Long Beach, California, real estate investment trust (REIT) typically acquires properties and then leases them to health care providers. Most of its lease contracts are long term agreements for 10 to 15 years.

The company owns and operates 31 hospitals, 173 long-term care facilities, 196 medical office buildings, and 30 other health care facilities. In all, HCPI has 554 properties in 44 states.

In terms of revenue generated, long-term care facilities account for about 24 percent, hospitals make up 27 percent, assisted living centers comprise 23 percent, medical office buildings make up 19 percent, other medical facilities make up 5 percent, and other income sources account for about 2 percent.

Founded in 1985, HCPI has a stock market capitalization of about $3.3 billion.

Dividend Yield   ☆ ☆ ☆ ☆
7.0 percent (2004)

Dividend Growth (past five years)   ☆
27 percent

Consistency   ☆ ☆ ☆ ☆
Increased dividends more than 10 consecutive years.

Financial Strength
Increased earnings per share only two of the past five years.
Increased revenues two of the past five years.

Financial Summary
Fiscal year ended: Dec. 31

	1998	1999	2000	2001	2002	2003	5-Year Growth (%)
Dividends/share ($)	1.31	1.39	1.47	1.55	1.63	1.66	27
Earnings/share ($)	1.23	1.11	1.07	.90	.97	1.07	—
Revenue ($millions)	162	225	330	333	360	400	147
Dividend yield (%)	7.5	10.1	10.7	8.6	8.0	8.0	—

5-year stock growth (mid-1999 to mid-2004): 92 percent ($13 to $25)

NSTAR

800 Boylston St.
Boston, MA 02199
617-424-2000

NYSE: NST
www.nstaronline.com

Chairman, CEO, and President: Thomas J. May

Current Yield	4.8 %	
Back-to-the-Future Yield	5-year 5.4%	10-year 8.5%

Rating

Dividend Yield	☆ ☆ ☆
Dividend Growth	
Consistency	☆ ☆ ☆
Financial Strength	☆ ☆ ☆
Total	9 points

BOSTON-BASED NSTAR, WHICH IS THE PARENT COMPANY OF BOSTON Edison, is the largest publicly-owned gas and electric utility company in Massachusetts. It has about 1.4 million residential customers in about eastern Massachusetts. In all, the company has 1.1. million electric customers in about 85 communities and 300,000 gas customers in about 55 communities.

Among the company's electric customers, residential customers generate about 38 percent of NSTAR's revenue, commercial customers account for 54 percent, industrial customers make up 7 percent, and other sources account for the final 1 percent. Among its gas customers, 61 percent of revenues come from residential customers, 25 percent from commercial customers, 10 percent from industrial customers, and 4 percent from off-line and contract customers.

NSTAR has non-utility subsidiaries in telecommunications and other energy-related fields.

NSTAR has been in business for more than a century (as Boston Edison). NSTAR has about 3,200 employees and a market capitalization of about $2.5 billion.

Dividend Yield ☆ ☆ ☆
4.8 percent (2004)

Dividend Growth (past five years)
15 percent

Consistency ☆ ☆ ☆
Increased dividends nine of the past 10 years.

Financial Strength ☆ ☆ ☆
Increased earnings per share eight consecutive years.
Increased revenues four of the past five years.

Financial Summary
Fiscal year ended: Dec. 31

	1998	1999	2000	2001	2002	2003	5-Year Growth (%)
Dividends/share ($)	1.90	1.96	2.02	2.08	2.13	2.18	15
Earnings/share ($)	2.76	2.77	3.19	3.27	3.38	3.50	27
Revenue ($billions)	1.62	1.85	2.70	3.19	2.72	2.91	80
Dividend yield (%)	4.7	4.8	4.9	5.0	4.9	4.9	—

5-year stock growth (mid-1999 to mid-2004): 14 percent ($42 to $48)

Bristol-Myers Squibb Company   50

345 Park Ave.
New York, NY 10154
212-546-4000

NYSE: BMY
www.bms.com

Chairman: Charles A. Heimbold
CEO: Peter A. Dolan

Current Yield	4.6%	
Back-to-the-Future Yield	5-year 1.6%	10-year 8.1%

Rating

Dividend Yield	☆ ☆ ☆
Dividend Growth	☆ ☆
Consistency	☆ ☆
Financial Strength	☆ ☆
Total	9 points

BRISTOL-MYERS SQUIBB PRODUCES A LONG LIST OF MEDICAL PRODUCTS designed to make your life a little less painful, such as the over-the-counter favorites Excedrin, Nuprin and Bufferin.

But Bristol-Myers makes most of its profits through prescription medications. Pharmaceuticals account for about 71 percent of its $21 billion in annual revenue.

Its Oncology Therapeutics Network accounts for about 11 percent of total revenue, Nutritional products make up 10 percent, and other healthcare products, such as consumer medicines and medical imaging products, account for 8 percent.

Among its leading nutritional suppliments are Enfamil, Prosobee, Nutramigen and Lactofree infant formula products, Isocal, Nutrament, Boost,

Choco Milk and Sustagen nutritional supplements, and Pusssz, Poly-Vi-sol, and Natalins vitamins.

The company's leading pharmaceuticals are used to treat cardiovascular and metabolic conditions, oncology, infectious diseases, including human immunodeficiency virus/acquired immune deficiency syndrome (HIV/AIDS), and psychiatric disorders.

Its leading medications include:

Pravachol ($2.8 billion in annual revenue). Used to treat high cholesterol

Plavix ($2.5 billion). A cardiovascular medicine used to prevent heart attacks.

Taxol ($934 million). Used in the treatment of refractory ovarian cancer and certain AIDS-related conditions, as well as in the treatment of breast cancer.

Paraplatin ($905 million). Used to treat ovarian cancer.

Avapro ($757 million). Used to treat hypertension and other cardiovascular conditions.

Bristol-Myers does a strong international business, with sales in more than 100 countries. Foreign sales account for about 29 percent of the company's total revenue.

Founded in 1887, Bristol-Myers merged with Squibb in 1989. The company has about 53,000 employees and a market capitalization of about $47 billion.

Dividend Yield ☆ ☆ ☆
4.6 percent (2004)

Dividend Growth (past five years) ☆ ☆
44 percent

Consistency ☆ ☆
Increased dividends eight of the past 10 years.

Financial Strength ☆ ☆
Increased earnings per share four of the past five years.
Increased revenues three of the past five years.

Financial Summary
Fiscal year ended: Dec. 31

	1998	1999	2000	2001	2002	2003	5-Year Growth (%)
Dividends/share ($)	.78	.86	.98	1.10	1.12	1.12	44
Earnings/share ($)	1.55	2.06	2.36	2.41	1.07	1.59	1
Revenue ($billions)	18.3	20.2	18.2	19.4	18.1	20.9	14
Dividend yield (%)	1.4	1.3	1.7	1.9	3.6	4.4	—

5-year stock growth (mid-1999 to mid-2004): -66 percent ($70 to $24)

FPL Group, Inc.

700 Universe Blvd.
Juno Beach, FL 33408
561-694-4697

NYSE: FPL
www.investor.fplgroup.com

Chairman and CEO: Lewis Hay

Current Yield	4.0%	
Back-to-the-Future Yield	5-year 4.7%	10-year 7.3%

Rating

Dividend Yield	☆ ☆ ☆
Dividend Growth	☆
Consistency	☆ ☆ ☆
Financial Strength	☆ ☆
Total	9 points

FPL GROUP, WHICH IS THE PARENT COMPANY OF FLORIDA POWER AND Light, is one of the nation's largest utility companies. The Juno Beach operation has about 4 million customers in Florida.

But Florida is not the only state where FPL sells energy. It claims a presence in 26 states, although the vast share of its revenue is generated in Florida. The company provides electricity to residential and commercial customers throughout Florida.

Residential customers make up about 56 percent of the company's operating revenues, commercial customers account for 37 percent, industrial customers make up about 3 percent, and other sources make up the final 4 percent.

FPL Group also has ownership interests in 42 wind power generation plants, with a combined capacity of approximately 2,719 mw (net ownership).

FPL is the nation's largest developer, owner and operator of wind power generating plants.

FLP Group has about 11,500 employees and a market capitalization of about $12 billion.

Dividend Yield   ☆ ☆ ☆
4.0 percent (2004)

Dividend Growth (past five years)   ☆
20 percent

Consistency   ☆ ☆ ☆
Increased dividends eight consecutive years.

Financial Strength   ☆ ☆
Increased earnings per share four of the past five years.
Increased revenues three of the past five years.

Financial Summary
Fiscal year ended: Dec. 31

	1998	1999	2000	2001	2002	2003	5-Year Growth (%)
Dividends/share ($)	2.00	2.08	2.16	2.24	2.32	2.40	20
Earnings/share ($)	3.85	4.07	4.14	4.62	4.02	4.89	27
Revenue ($billions)	6.66	6.44	7.08	8.48	8.31	9.63	45
Dividend yield (%)	3.2	3.9	4.1	3.9	4.1	3.9	—

5-year stock growth (mid-1999 to mid-2004): 24 percent ($55 to $68)

Lincoln National Corp. 52

1500 Market St., Suite 3900
Philadelphia, PA 19102
215-448-1453

NYSE: LNC
www.lfg.com

Chairman, CEO, and President: Jon A. Boscia

Current Yield	3.1%	
Back-to-the-Future Yield	5-year 2.9%	10-year 6.9%

Rating

Dividend Yield	☆ ☆
Dividend Growth	☆
Consistency	☆ ☆ ☆ ☆
Financial Strength	☆ ☆
Total	9 points

LINCOLN NATIONAL COVERS THE GAMUT OF INSURANCE AND RETIREMENT products, including annuities, life insurance, 401(k) and 403(b) plans, 529 college savings plans, mutual funds, managed accounts, institutional investment services, and financial planning and advisory services.

The Philadelphia operation divides its operations into four business groups:

Lincoln Retirement (40 percent of revenues). The firm provides tax-deferred investment growth and retirement income through fixed and variable annuities.

Life insurance (38 percent). The company provides a broad range of life insurance products.

Investment management (11 percent). Lincoln offers investment products and services to both individual and institutional investors.

Lincoln UK (6 percent). Headquartered in Barnwood, Gloucester, England, Lincoln UK oversees the company's insurance business in the UK.

Founded in 1905, Lincoln National has about 6,800 employees and a market capitalization of $7.8 billion.

Dividend Yield   ☆ ☆
3.1 percent (2004)

Dividend Growth (past five years)   ☆
31 percent

Consistency   ☆ ☆ ☆ ☆
Increased dividends more than 15 consecutive years.

Financial Strength   ☆ ☆
Increased earnings per share three of the past five years.
Increased total income two of the past five years.

Financial Summary
Fiscal year ended: Dec. 31

	1998	1999	2000	2001	2002	2003	5-Year Growth (%)
Dividends/share ($)	1.04	1.10	1.16	1.22	1.30	1.36	31
Earnings/share ($)	2.67	3.14	3.68	3.57	2.54	3.00	12
Income ($billions)	6.01	6.8	6.85	6.38	4.64	5.28	—
Dividend yield (%)	2.4	2.4	2.9	2.6	3.2	3.9	—

5-year stock growth (mid-1999 to mid-2004): 2 percent ($44 to $45).

Genuine Parts Company 53

2999 Circle 75 Parkway
Atlanta, GA 30339
770-953-1700

NYSE: GPC
www.genpt.com

Chairman and CEO: Larry L. Prince
President: Thomas C. Gallagher

Current Yield	3.2%	
Back-to-the-Future Yield	5-year 4.1%	10-year 4.9%

Rating

Dividend Yield	☆ ☆
Dividend Growth	☆
Consistency	☆ ☆ ☆ ☆
Financial Strength	☆ ☆
Total	9 points

GENUINE PARTS IS NORTH AMERICA'S LARGEST AUTO PARTS DISTRIBUTOR, with about 900 stores in the U.S., Canada and Mexico, and 5,000 independent distributors. The company sells about 300,000 different auto parts, primarily through the NAPA (National Auto Parts Association) network.

But auto parts account for only about 53 percent of the company's total revenue. The Atlanta-based operation also has three other key business segments:

Industrial products (27 percent of revenue). Through its Motion Industries subsidiary, Genuine is North America's largest distributor of industrial maintenance, repair, and operation replacement parts. Motion sells bearings; mechanical, industrial automation, electrical, pneumatic, and hydraulic power replacement parts; hose and rubber products and industrial supply products. The company has more than 450 operations including nine distribution centers and serves more than 150,000 customers including automotive, chemical, food, beverage, wood and lumber, iron, oil, pulp and paper, steel and textile industries.

Office products (17 percent). Through its S. P. Richards subsidiary, the company distributes more than 30,000 business products to a network of more than 7,000 resellers in the U.S. and Canada.

Electrical products (3 percent). Through its EIS subsidiary, the company supplies and manufactures a broad range of products for electronic and electrical apparatus, including insulating and conductive materials, assembly tools, test equipment and customized parts.

Founded in 1928, Genuine Parts has about 31,000 employees and a market capitalization of about $7 billion.

Dividend Yield ☆ ☆
3.2 percent (2004)

Dividend Growth (past five years) ☆
19 percent

Consistency ☆ ☆ ☆ ☆
Increased dividends 47 consecutive years.

Financial Strength ☆ ☆
Increased earnings per share three of the past five years.
Increased revenues four of the past five years.

Financial Summary
Fiscal year ended: Dec. 31

	1998	1999	2000	2001	2002	2003	5-Year Growth (%)
Dividends/share ($)	.99	1.04	1.10	1.14	1.16	1.18	19
Earnings/share ($)	1.98	2.11	2.20	2.08	2.10	2.03	3
Revenue ($billions)	6.61	7.98	8.37	8.22	8.26	8.45	28
Dividend yield (%)	2.9	3.5	5.0	3.8	3.5	3.7	—

5-year stock growth (mid-1999 to mid-2004): 36 percent ($28 to $38)

Pitney Bowes, Inc.

Walter H. Wheeler, Jr. Dr.
Stamford, CT 06926
203-356-5000

NYSE: PBI
www.pitneybowes.com

Chairman and CEO: Michael J. Critelli

Current Yield	2.8%	
Back-to-the-Future Yield	**5-year** **2.1%**	**10-year** **6.4%**

Rating

Dividend Yield	☆
Dividend Growth	☆
Consistency	☆ ☆ ☆ ☆
Financial Strength	☆ ☆ ☆
Total	**9 points**

COME RAIN, SLEET OR SNOW, THE MAIL MUST GO THROUGH, AND FOR THE past 80 years, Pitney Bowes has done its best to make that happen. Pitney is the world's leading maker of postage meters and other mail and document management systems. It boasts more than 2 million business customers worldwide.

The company typically leases postage metering equipment to its customers and sells supplies. It also offers related services to its metering customers. In addition to postage meters, Pitney provides mailing machines, address hygiene software, letter and parcel scales, mail openers, mail room furniture, folders, and paper handling and shipping equipment.

It also offers facilities management services, assisting companies with a variety of support functions, such as correspondence mail, copy centers, fax services, electronic printing, reprographics management, high volume automated mail center management and related activities. Target customers are large industrial companies, banking and financial institutions, and services organizations such as law firms and accounting firms.

The company breaks its operations into three key segments:

Global mailing (69 percent of revenue). The company rents and sells meters and mailing equipment in the U.S. and Europe.

Enterprise Solutions (28 percent). The firm provides mail room and document management services and sells software systems.

Capital services (3 percent). This arm of the company does the financing for Pitney's equipment leasing business.

Pitney Bowes has about 33,000 employees and a market capitalization of about $10 billion.

Dividend Yield ☆
2.8 percent (2004)

Dividend Growth (past five years) ☆
33 percent

Consistency ☆ ☆ ☆ ☆
Increased dividends 21 consecutive years.

Financial Strength ☆ ☆ ☆
Increased earnings per share four of the past five years.
Increased revenues four of the past five years.

Financial Summary
Fiscal year ended: Dec. 31

	1998	1999	2000	2001	2002	2003	5-Year Growth (%)
Dividends/share ($)	.90	1.02	1.14	1.16	1.18	1.20	33
Earnings/share ($)	2.03	2.31	2.44	2.25	2.37	2.41	19
Revenue ($billions)	4.22	4.43	3.88	4.12	4.41	4.58	9
Dividend yield (%)	1.7	1.7	2.9	3.0	3.1	3.3	—

5-year stock growth (mid-1999 to mid-2004): -28 percent ($60 to $43)

Procter & Gamble Company

1 Procter & Gamble Plaza
Cincinnati, OH 45202
513-983-1100

NYSE: PG
www.pg.com

President and CEO: Alan Lafley

Current Yield	2.0%	
Back-to-the-Future Yield	5-year 1.9%	10-year 6.9%

Rating

Dividend Yield	
Dividend Growth	☆ ☆
Consistency	☆ ☆ ☆ ☆
Financial Strength	☆ ☆ ☆
Total	9 points

FROM DISH SOAPS AND LAUNDRY DETERGENTS TO COFFEE AND COSMETICS, Procter & Gamble has its hands in the private lives of millions of consumers. In all, the Cincinnati operation puts more than 300 product brands on the market.

But P&G has spread its Cheer (and Tide) around the world. The company sells its soaps, foods and beauty care products in more than 140 countries. About 46 percent of the company's revenue is generated outside of North America.

Detergents and other home care products account for about 27 percent of the company's annual revenue. In addition to Tide and Cheer, P&G makes Ariel, Downy, Dawn, Joy, Gain, Dash, Bold, Cascade, Mr. Clean, Febreze, Bounce, Era, Dreft, Daz, Rindex and a number of other cleaning products.

Its other product segments include:

Baby and family care (20 percent of revenue). Products include Bounty, Pampers, Puffs, Luvs, Charmin, and Kandoo.

Beauty care (33 percent). The company makes a wide range of beauty care products, including Cover Girl, Vidal Sassoon, Secret, Clearasil, Noxzema, Coast, Lava, Oil of Olay, Safeguard, Zest, Max Factor, Sure, Head & Shoulders, Old Spice, Camay, Always, Whisper, Tampax, and Pert.

Snacks and beverages (3.5 percent). Leading products include Folgers, Pringles and Millstone.

Health care (13 percent). The company makes Crest, Scope, Vicks, Prilosec OTC, Metamucil, Pepto-Bismol, Fixodent, and a number of prescription and over-the-counter medications.

Founded in 1837 by William Procter and James Gamble, the company is the world's leading producer of soaps and cosmetics. P&G has managed to maintain its strong market position through a relentless advertising approach. For many years, the company was TV's biggest advertiser.

P&G has 98,000 employees and a market capitalization of about $140 billion.

Dividend Yield
2.0 percent (2004)

Dividend Growth (past five years) ☆ ☆
63 percent

Consistency ☆ ☆ ☆ ☆
Increased dividends more than 15 consecutive years.

Financial Strength ☆ ☆ ☆
Increased earnings per share four of the past five years.
Increased revenues four of the past five years.

Financial Summary
Fiscal year ended: June 30

	1999	2000	2001	2002	2003	2004	5-Year Growth (%)
Dividends/share ($)	.57	.64	.70	.76	.82	.93	63
Earnings/share ($)	1.43	1.48	1.03	1.55	1.85	2.33	63
Revenue ($billions)	38.1	40.0	39.2	40.2	43.4	51.4	17
Dividend yield (%)	1.3	1.5	2.1	1.9	1.9	2.1	—

5-year stock growth (mid-1999 to mid-2004): 20 percent ($51 to $56)

Alltel Corp.

One Allied Drive
Little Rock, AR 72202
877-446-3628

NYSE: AT
www.alltel.com

Chairman: Joe T. Ford
CEO and President: Scott T. Ford

Current Yield	2.8%	
Back-to-the-Future Yield	5-year 2.0%	10-year 5.7%

Rating

Dividend Yield	☆
Dividend Growth	☆
Consistency	☆ ☆ ☆ ☆
Financial Strength	☆ ☆ ☆
Total	**9 points**

ALLTEL CORP. PROVIDES LOCAL, LONG-DISTANCE, WIRELESS AND INTERNET services to nearly 13 million customers in 26 states.

The company also publishes telephone directories for its affiliates and other independent telephone companies. The Little Rock operation also offers billing, customer service and other data processing and outsourcing services to other telecommunications companies.

Alltel has grown quickly through a series of acquisitions, including Liberty Cell and Alliant Communications in 1999. Its customer base has grown from 2.5 million customers in 1996 to 12.8 million in 2004.

The company's growth has been aided by the boom in the cellular phone market. Alltel provides wireless services to about eight million customers in 23 states. It owns the majority interest in wireless operations in 88 metropolitan areas and about 150 rural markets. It also owns minority interest in wireless operations in 51 other markets, including Chicago and Houston.

Wireless services account for about 58 percent of Alltel's revenue, regular phone service makes up 30 percent, and communications support services account for about 12 percent.

Alltel has about 20,000 employees and a market capitalization of about $16 million.

Dividend Yield ☆
2.8 percent (2004)

Dividend Growth (past five years) ☆
20 percent

Consistency ☆ ☆ ☆ ☆
Increased dividends 43 consecutive years.

Financial Strength ☆ ☆ ☆
Increased earnings per share four of the past five years.
Increased revenues four of the past five years.

Financial Summary
Fiscal year ended: Dec. 31

	1998	1999	2000	2001	2002	2003	5-Year Growth (%)
Dividends/share ($)	1.18	1.24	1.29	1.33	1.37	1.42	20
Earnings/share ($)	2.09	2.39	2.70	2.67	2.92	3.01	44
Revenue ($billions)	5.19	6.3	7.07	7.6	7.98	7.98	54
Dividend yield (%)	2.6	1.8	2.1	2.3	2.8	3.0	—

5-year stock growth (mid-1999 to mid-2004): -23 percent ($71 to $55)

Merck & Company

57

One Merck Drive
P.O. Box 100
Whitehouse Station, NJ 08889
908-423-1000

NYSE: MRK
www.merck.com

Chairman, CEO, and President: Raymond V. Gilmartin

Current Yield	4.8%	
Back-to-the-Future Yield	5-year 2.0%	10-year 8.7%

Rating

Dividend Yield	☆ ☆ ☆
Dividend Growth	☆ ☆
Consistency	☆ ☆ ☆ ☆
Financial Strength	
Total	9 points

MERCK IS STILL ONE OF THE WORLD'S LEADING PHARMACEUTICAL manufacturers, but it is a much leaner company now than it was a couple of years ago. In late 1993, Merck spun off its Medco subsidiary, a medical distribution operation that accounted for about 50 percent of Merck's revenues, but a much smaller percent of its profits.

Merck had acquired Medco in 1993 in hopes of integrating it into its operations. But Medco never proved to be a good fit, and ultimately detracted from Merck's chief focus, which is to research, develop, manufacture and market medications in a broad range of areas.

Among the leading drugs offered by Merck are:

Zocor, a cholesterol medication, which is among the world's top selling drugs

Mevacor, another leading cholesterol medication

Fosamax, an osteoporosis medication

Singulair, one of the leading asthma medicines in every country in which it is sold.

The company was forced in 2004 to take one of its leading sellers off the market. Vioxx, a leading arthritis medication launched in 1999, was found in clinical studies to increase the possibility of heart attacks and strokes. Pulling the product was a huge blow for Merck, costing the company about $700 million in annual sales. Merck stock dropped more than 30 percent after Vioxx sales were suspended.

Merck's biggest selling segment is its cholesterol treatments (which the company categorizes as atherosclerosis medications). Those medicines, including Zocor and Mevacor, account for about 23 percent of the company's total revenue. Cardiovascular medications, which are used to treat heart problems and hypertension, account for about 15 percent.

Other leading segments include anti-inflammatory medications, 12 percent; osteoporosis, 12 percent; respiratory, 9 percent; vaccines and biologicals, 5 percent; and anti-bacterial and anti-fungal, 4 percent.

Merck has operations in about 20 countries, with sales in more than 100 countries. Sales outside the U.S. account for about 41 percent of total sales.

Founded in 1881, Merck has about 63,000 employees and a market capitalization of about $100 billion.

Dividend Yield ☆ ☆ ☆
4.8 percent (2004)

Dividend Growth (past five years) ☆ ☆
53 percent

Consistency ☆ ☆ ☆ ☆
Increased dividends 23 consecutive years.

Financial Strength
Increased earnings per share three of the past five years, but recently took a big hit in earnings when Vioxx sales were suspended.

Increased revenues five of the past five years.

Financial Summary
Fiscal year ended: Dec. 31

	1998	1999	2000	2001	2002	2003	5-Year Growth (%)
Dividends/share ($)	.95	1.10	1.21	1.37	1.41	1.45	53
Earnings/share ($)	2.15	2.45	2.90	3.14	3.14	2.92	36
Revenue ($billions)	15.1	17.3	20	21.2	21.4	22.5	49
Dividend yield (%)	1.5	1.5	1.6	1.9	2.6	2.7	—

5-year stock growth (late 1999 to late 2004): -65 percent ($77 to $27)

Coca-Cola Company

58

One Coca-Cola Plaza
Atlanta, GA 30313
404-676-2121

NYSE: KO
www.coca-cola.com

Chairman and CEO: Neville Isdell

Current Yield	2.4%	
Back-to-the-Future Yield	5-year 1.6%	10-year 4.1%

Rating

Dividend Yield	
Dividend Growth	☆ ☆
Consistency	☆ ☆ ☆ ☆
Financial Strength	☆ ☆ ☆
Total	9 points

HAVE A COKE AND A CHECK. THE COCA-COLA COMPANY HAS INCREASED ITS dividend to shareholders for 42 consecutive years.

The Atlanta-based beverage maker has grown far beyond Coke and Diet Coke. It is the leading soft drink maker in the world, with sales in nearly 200 countries on every continent. Coke is one of the most recognizable brand names in the world. Coke's international sales account for about 69 percent of its revenue and 80 percent of its profit.

Coca-Cola produces nearly 400 brands of beverages. But aside from Coke-related merchandise, the company offers very little outside of the non-alcoholic beverage segment. Despite its narrow focus, however, Coke has managed to grow steadily based on its ability to bring a series of new beverages to the market—and to acquire other successful brands.

The company's leading beverage brands (other than Coke) include Sprite, Barq's, Mr. PiBB, Fanta, Dasani, Evian, Danone, Powerade, Minute Maid and Five Alive. It also makes Cherry Coke, Vanilla Coke, Mello Yello, TAB, and Fresca. In certain countries, Coke also has marketing rights for Schweppes, Canada Dry, Dr. Pepper and Crush.

Coke's latest major offering is C2, which tastes very similar to Coke, but has half the calories and half the carbohydrates of real Coke.

Founded in 1886, Coke has about 49,000 employees and a market capitalization of about $106 billion.

Dividend Yield
2.4 percent (2004)

Dividend Growth (past five years)   ☆ ☆
47 percent

Consistency   ☆ ☆ ☆ ☆
Increased dividends 42 consecutive years.

Financial Strength   ☆ ☆ ☆
Increased earnings per share four of the past five years.
Increased revenues four of the past five years.

Financial Summary
Fiscal year ended: Dec. 31

	1998	1999	2000	2001	2002	2003	5-Year Growth (%)
Dividends/share ($)	.60	.64	.68	.72	.80	.88	47
Earnings/share ($)	1.42	1.30	1.48	1.60	1.65	1.95	37
Revenue ($billions)	18.8	19.8	20.5	17.5	19.6	21.0	12
Dividend yield (%)	0.8	1.0	1.2	1.5	1.6	2.0	—

5-year stock growth (mid-1999 to mid-2004): -28 percent ($60 to $43)

Healthcare Realty Trust

59

3310 West End Ave., Suite 700
Nashville, TN 37203
615-269-8175

NYSE: HR
www.healthcarerealty.com

Chairman and CEO: David R. Emery

Current Yield	6.8%	
Back-to-the-Future Yield	5-year 13.2%	10-year 12.3%

Rating

Dividend Yield	☆ ☆ ☆ ☆
Dividend Growth	☆
Consistency	☆ ☆ ☆
Financial Strength	
Total	8 points

HEALTHCARE REALTY IS A REAL ESTATE INVESTMENT TRUST (REIT) THAT focuses largely on outpatient medical care facilities. The company also owns and operates about 60 hospitals and 30 assisted care facilities, but it has turned most of its attention recently to outpatient centers.

In all, the Nashville operation owns and operates about 260 properties—13 million square feet of total space—in 32 states from coast to coast. It also provides property management services for more than 100 other healthcare-related properties.

Its biggest tenants are HealthSouth Corp., which account for about 13 percent of Healthcare Realty's annual revenue, and HCA, which accounts for 11 percent.

Because of growing financial pressures in the health care industry, outpatient treatment has been the fastest growing segment of the industry—and

Healthcare Realty is betting that that trend will continue. It has made several acquisitions recently to bolster its holdings, including the 2004 acquisition of 20 medical office buildings from Baylor Health Care System in Dallas.

Founded in 1992, Healthcare Realty has only about 200 employees and a stock market capitalization of about $1.6 billion.

Dividend Yield   ☆ ☆ ☆ ☆
6.8 percent (2004)

Dividend Growth (past five years)   ☆
19 percent

Consistency   ☆ ☆ ☆
Increased dividends nine of the past 10 years.

Financial Strength
Increased earnings per share only two of the past five years.
Increased revenues two of the past five years.

Financial Summary
Fiscal year ended: Dec. 31

	1998	1999	2000	2001	2002	2003	5-Year Growth (%)
Dividends/share ($)	2.07	2.15	2.23	2.31	2.39	2.47	19
Earnings/share ($)	1.63	1.99	1.82	1.81	1.84	1.66	1
Revenue ($millions)	91	185	193	192	192	192	110
Dividend yield (%)	10.5	10.9	12.3	9.1	8.0	8.0	—

5-year stock growth (mid-1999 to mid-2004): 90 percent ($20 to $38)

Mack-Cali Realty Corp.

60

11 Commerce Drive
Cranford, NJ 07016
908-272-8000

NYSE: CLI
www.mack-cali.com

Chairman: William L. Mack
President and CEO: Mitchell E. Hersh

Current Yield	6.1%	
Back-to-the-Future Yield	5-year 8.8%	10-year 15.6%

Rating

Dividend Yield	☆ ☆ ☆ ☆
Dividend Growth	☆
Consistency	☆ ☆ ☆
Financial Strength	
Total	8 points

MACK-CALI REALTY CORP. IS A REAL ESTATE INVESTMENT TRUST (REIT) THAT focuses primarily on office buildings, although it does own a few other types of commercial properties.

In all, the New Jersey operation owns and operates 263 commercial properties encompassing about 28 million square feet. That includes nearly 250 office buildings, six industrial and warehouse buildings and two stand-alone retail properties. The company also has ownership interests in a 350-room hotel. It recently announced an agreement to acquire four more buildings from AT&T.

Mack-Cali also owns additional land that could be used to develop up to eight million square feet of commercial space.

Most of the company's properties are located in the Northeast. In all, it has properties in nine states and Washington, D.C.

Founded more than 50 years ago, Mack-Cali Realty reorganized as a REIT in 1994 when it made its initial public stock offering. The company has about 335 employees and a stock market capitalization of about $2.5 billion.

Dividend Yield ☆ ☆ ☆ ☆
6.1 percent (2004)

Dividend Growth (past five years) ☆
20 percent

Consistency ☆ ☆ ☆
Increased dividends nine of the past 10 years.

Financial Strength
Increased earnings only two of the past five years.
Increased revenues four of the past five years.

Financial Summary
Fiscal year ended: Dec. 31

	1998	1999	2000	2001	2002	2003	5-Year Growth (%)
Dividends/share ($)	2.10	2.26	2.38	2.46	2.50	2.52	20
Earnings/share ($)	2.11	2.04	3.10	2.32	2.43	2.43	15
Revenue ($millions)	494	544	560	569	564	586	19
Dividend yield (%)	6.2	7.9	9.1	8.7	7.9	7.3	—

5-year stock growth (mid-1999 to mid-2004): 61 percent ($28 to $45)

Progress Energy

411 Fayetteville St.
Raleigh, NC 27602
800-662-7232

NYSE: PGN
www.progress-energy.com

Chairman: William Cavanaugh, III
CEO and President: Robert B. McGehee

Current Yield	5.5%	
Back-to-the-Future Yield	5-year 5.8%	10-year 8.6%

Rating

Dividend Yield	☆ ☆ ☆ ☆
Dividend Growth	
Consistency	☆ ☆ ☆ ☆
Financial Strength	
Total	8 points

PROGRESS ENERGY IS THE PARENT COMPANY OF FLORIDA PROGRESS (formerly Florida Power Company) and CP&L Energy (formerly Carolina Power & Light Company). Progress provides electricity for parts of Florida, North Carolina and South Carolina.

The company serves nearly 3 million residential customers, with a generation capacity of more than 24,000 megawatts. About 35 percent of its revenues from its electric service comes from residential customers, 24 percent comes from commercial customers, 18 percent comes from industrial customers, and 24 percent from related services.

Although its electrical service provides the vast share of its revenues, Progress also operates in several other business segments. Its Fuels business segment is involved in natural gas drilling and production, coal terminal services, coal mining, synthetic fuel production, fuel transportation and delivery. Through its Rail Services business segment, Progress is engaged in various rail and railcar related services.

The Raleigh, NC operation is also involved in telecommunication services.

Progress Energy has about 15,000 employees and a market capitalization of about $10 billion.

Dividend Yield ☆ ☆ ☆ ☆
5.5 percent (2004)

Dividend Growth (past five years)
15 percent

Consistency ☆ ☆ ☆ ☆
Increased dividends 10 consecutive years.

Financial Strength
Increased earnings per share only two of the past five years.
Increased revenues four of the past five years.

Financial Summary
Fiscal year ended: Dec. 31

	1998	1999	2000	2001	2002	2003	5-Year Growth (%)
Dividends/share ($)	1.96	2.02	2.08	2.14	2.18	2.26	15
Earnings/share ($)	2.75	2.55	2.34	3.43	3.84	3.41	24
Revenue ($billions)	3.13	3.36	4.12	8.46	7.95	8.74	179
Dividend yield (%)	4.5	5.2	5.8	5.0	4.8	5.3	—

5-year stock growth (mid-1999 to mid-2004): 13 percent ($38 to $43)

Consolidated Edison, Inc.

62

4 Irving Place
New York, NY 1003
212-460-3903

NYSE: ED
www.coned.com

Chairman, CEO, and President: Eugene R. McGrath

Current Yield	5.9%	
Back-to-the-Future Yield	5-year 5.2%	10-year 8.1%

Rating

Dividend Yield	☆ ☆ ☆ ☆
Dividend Growth	
Consistency	☆ ☆ ☆ ☆
Financial Strength	
Total	8 points

CONSOLIDATED EDISON IS ONE OF THE NATION'S LARGEST UTILITIES, providing electricity and natural gas to much of New York City and neighboring Westchester County—an area of about 660 square miles.

Con Edison operates in three principal business segments, including:

Electric Supply (78 percent of operating revenue). Con Ed is the leading supplier of electricity in the New York City area. Most of the electricity sold by Con Edison of New York to its customers is purchased under firm power contracts or through the wholesale electricity market administered by the New York Independent System Operator (NYISO).

Gas Sales (16 percent). About half of the natural gas delivered to Con Ed customers is comes from the company while the other half comes from other suppliers.

Steam Sales (6 percent). Con Edison of New York sells steam in Manhattan south of 96th Street, mostly to large office buildings, apartment houses and hospitals. About 52 percent of the steam sold by Con Edison of New York is produced in the company's steam-only generating stations; 36 percent is produced in the company's steam/electric generating stations, where it is first used to generate electricity; and 12 percent is purchased from other suppliers.

Incorporated in 1884, Con Edison has about 14,000 employees and a market capitalization of about $8.8 billion.

Dividend Yield ☆ ☆ ☆ ☆
5.9 percent (2004)

Dividend Growth (past five years)
6 percent

Consistency ☆ ☆ ☆ ☆
Increased dividends more than 15 consecutive years.

Financial Strength
Increased earnings per share two of the past five years.
Increased revenues four of the past five years.

Financial Summary
Fiscal year ended: Dec. 31

	1998	1999	2000	2001	2002	2003	5-Year Growth (%)
Dividends/share ($)	2.12	2.14	2.18	2.20	2.22	2.24	6
Earnings/share ($)	3.04	3.13	2.74	3.21	3.13	2.83	—
Revenue ($billions)	7.1	7.5	9.4	9.6	8.5	9.8	38
Dividend yield (%)	4.6	4.9	6.6	5.7	5.3	5.5	—

5-year stock growth (mid-1999 to mid-2004): -10 percent ($45 to $41)

Equity Residential Properties Trust 63

Two North Riverside Plaza
Chicago, IL 60606
312-466-4083

NYSE: EQR
www.equityapartments.com

Chairman: Samuel Zell
CEO: Bruce W. Duncan

Current Yield	5.9%	
Back-to-the-Future Yield	5-year 8.0%	10-year 11.3%

Rating

Dividend Yield	☆ ☆ ☆ ☆
Dividend Growth	☆
Consistency	☆ ☆ ☆
Financial Strength	
Total	8 points

Equity Residential Properties owns condos, apartment complexes and other residential properties throughout a broad geographic area. The Chicago-based real estate investment trust (REIT) owns or operates nearly a thousand properties with a total of about 208,000 rental units in 34 states.

It is the nation's largest publicly-traded owner and operator of multi-family housing.

The company's primary concentration of properties is in the Mid-Atlantic region, as well as Texas, Florida and Arizona. It focuses on metropolitan area properties with at least 200 units. About 29 percent of its properties are in the Southwest, about 30 percent are in the East and Northeast, and 14 percent are in the Pacific region.

The company's offerings include unfurnished apartments of a variety of sizes and styles, furnished corporate suites and condos in a wide range of prices.

Founded in 1993, Equity Residential has about 6,000 employees and a stock market capitalization of about $8.5 billion.

Dividend Yield
5.9 percent (2004)

Dividend Growth (past five years)
27 percent

Consistency
Increased dividends nine of the past 10 years.

Financial Strength
Increased earnings per share only two of the past five years.
Increased revenues two of the past five years.

Financial Summary
Fiscal year ended: Dec. 31

	1998	1999	2000	2001	2002	2003	5-Year Growth (%)
Dividends/share ($)	1.36	1.47	1.58	1.68	1.73	1.73	27
Earnings/share ($)	.82	.80	.99	.86	.82	.53	—
Revenue ($millions)	1.29	1.71	1.96	2.08	1.97	1.08	—
Dividend yield (%)	6.2	6.6	6.6	6.1	6.6	6.5	—

5-year stock growth (mid-1999 to mid-2004): 41 percent ($22 to $31)

SBC Communications, Inc.

64

175 E. Houston
San Antonio, TX 78205
210-821-4105

NYSE: SBC
www.sbc.com

Chairman and CEO: Edward E. Whitacre, Jr.

Current Yield	4.7%	
Back-to-the-Future Yield	5-year 3.1%	10-year 6.4%

Rating

Dividend Yield	☆ ☆ ☆
Dividend Growth	☆ ☆
Consistency	☆ ☆ ☆
Financial Strength	
Total	8 points

SBC COMMUNICATIONS IS ONE OF THE WORLD'S LARGEST TELECOM-munications companies, with operations in the U.S. and more than 25 other countries.

The company offers local exchange services, wireless communications, long-distance services, internet services, telecommunications equipment, and directory advertising and publishing. In 2004 it also began offering satellite television services through an agreement with EchoStar Communications Corp.

The San Antonio operation breaks its service offerings into four primary categories:

Wire line. The company offers land and wire-based services to customers in 13 states, including Arkansas, California, Connecticut, Illinois, Indiana, Kansas, Michigan, Missouri, Nevada, Ohio, Oklahoma, Texas, and Wisconsin.

Wireless. The company holds a stake in Cingular Wireless, which provides radio-wave-based wireless services.

Directories. SBC does directory publishing and advertising.

International. The company owns a stake in communications companies in more than 25 other countries.

SBC was formed in 1984 along with the other Baby Bell companies as part of the break-up of AT&T. The company has about 170,000 employees and a market capitalization of about $80 billion.

Dividend Yield   ☆ ☆ ☆
4.7 percent (2004)

Dividend Growth (past five years)   ☆ ☆
46 percent

Consistency   ☆ ☆ ☆
Increased dividends nine of the past 10 years.

Financial Strength
Increased earnings per share only two of the past five years.
Increased revenues three of the past five years.

Financial Summary
Fiscal year ended: Dec. 31

	1998	1999	2000	2001	2002	2003	5-Year Growth (%)
Dividends/share ($)	.94	.97	1.01	1.02	1.07	1.37	46
Earnings/share ($)	2.24	1.90	2.27	2.07	2.23	1.80	—
Revenue ($billions)	46.2	49.5	53.3	54.3	51.8	40.8	—
Dividend yield (%)	2.2	1.8	2.2	2.4	3.5	5.8	—

5-year stock growth (mid-1999 to mid-2004): -49 percent ($51 to $26)

Telefonos de Mexico S.A.

65

Parque Via 190
Colonia Cuauhtemoc, 06599 Mexico, D.F., Mexico

NYSE: TMX
www.telmex.com

Chairman: Carlos Slim Helu
CEO: Jaimie Chico Pardo

Current Yield	4.2%	
Back-to-the-Future Yield	5-year 3.0%	10-year 4.1%

Rating

Dividend Yield	☆ ☆ ☆
Dividend Growth	☆ ☆
Consistency	☆
Financial Strength	☆ ☆
Total	8 points

TELEFONOS DE MEXICO, KNOWN AS TELMEX, IS NOT ONLY MEXICO'S largest telephone company, it is the country's largest publicly-traded company.

Telmex has a virtual monopoly on phone service in most of Mexico. It is the country's only nationwide provider of fixed-line telephone services and the leading provider of fixed local and long distance telephone services as well as Internet access in Mexico.

The company also offers other telecommunications and telecommunications-related services, such as connectivity, Internet services, directory services, interconnection services to other carriers and paging services.

About 47 percent of its revenue comes from local phone service, 34 percent comes from long distance service, 15 percent comes from interconnection services to other carriers, and 4 percent is generated by yellow pages publishing, equipment sales and other services.

The company has about 15 million phone lines in service in 21,000 communities and about 1.2 million Internet customers

Telmex, which trades on the NYSE, has about 64,000 employees and a market capitalization of about $20 billion

Dividend Yield ☆ ☆ ☆
4.2 percent (2004)

Dividend Growth (past five years) ☆ ☆
48 percent

Consistency ☆
Increased dividends seven of the past 10 years.

Financial Strength ☆ ☆
Increased earnings per share four of the past five years.
Increased revenues three of the past five years.

Financial Summary
Fiscal year ended: Dec. 31

	1998	1999	2000	2001	2002	2003	5-Year Growth (%)
Dividends/share ($)	.75	.76	.93	.93	1.07	1.11	48
Earnings/share ($)	2.10	3.50	3.56	3.80	2.88	3.04	45
Revenue ($billions)	7.9	10.1	10.7	12.1	10.9	10.4	32
Dividend yield (%)	3.0	2.0	1.7	2.7	3.2	3.6	—

5-year stock growth (mid-1999 to mid-2004): 50 percent ($22 to $33)

New Jersey Resources Corp. 66

1415 Wyckoff Road
Wall, NJ 07719
908-938-1480

NYSE: NJR
www.njliving.com

Chairman and CEO: Laurence M. Downes

Current Yield	3.4%	
Back-to-the-Future Yield	5-year 5.1%	10-year 8.1%

Rating

Dividend Yield	☆ ☆
Dividend Growth	
Consistency	☆ ☆ ☆
Financial Strength	☆ ☆ ☆
Total	8 points

NEW JERSEY RESOURCES IS THE HOLDING COMPANY OF NEW JERSEY GAS CO., which provides natural gas for about 450,000 customers in the New Jersey counties of Monmouth and Ocean and surrounding areas.

The company also owns New Jersey Natural Energy, which provides retail and wholesale natural gas and related services to customers in 17 states.

Residential customers account for about 57 percent of the company's operating revenue, commercial customers account for about 13 percent, and transportation accounts for about 5 percent. Revenues from other operations make up the other 25 percent.

In addition to its natural gas services, New Jersey Resources also operates a subsidiary that provides bulk natural gas, storage and fuel management.

The company's primary retail utility business is concentrated in a well-populated area of New Jersey along the Atlantic coast. Steady growth of the area's population has helped New Jersey Resources grow quickly over the past decade. The company has posted 12 consecutive years of increased earnings per share.

New Jersey Resources has about 550 utility employees and a market capitalization of about $1.1 billion.

Dividend Yield ☆ ☆
3.4 percent (2004)

Dividend Growth (past five years)
14 percent

Consistency ☆ ☆ ☆
Increased dividends eight consecutive years.

Financial Strength ☆ ☆ ☆
Increased earnings per share 12 consecutive years.
Increased revenue four of the past five years.

Financial Summary
Fiscal year ended: Sept. 30

	1998	1999	2000	2001	2002	2003	5-Year Growth (%)
Dividends/share ($)	1.09	1.12	1.15	1.17	1.20	1.24	14
Earnings/share ($)	1.55	1.67	1.82	1.95	2.09	2.38	54
Revenue ($billions)	.71	.90	1.16	2.05	1.83	2.54	258
Dividend yield (%)	4.6	4.5	4.4	4.2	3.9	3.7	—

5-year stock growth (late-1999 to late-2004): 52 percent ($27 to $41)

Mercury General Corp. 67

4484 Wilshire Blvd.
Los Angeles, CA 90010
323-937-1060

NYSE: MCY
www.mercuryinsurance.com

Chairman and CEO: George Joseph

Current Yield	2.9%	
Back-to-the-Future Yield	5-year 4.2%	10-year 9.8%

Rating

Dividend Yield	☆
Dividend Growth	☆ ☆ ☆
Consistency	☆ ☆ ☆ ☆
Financial Strength	
Total	8 points

MERCURY GENERAL MAY BE A LITTLE KNOWN NAME IN MOST STATES, BUT IN California it is one of the leading carriers of automobile insurance for private passenger and commercial motorists.

Mercury does about 84 percent of its business in California. It does not have a presence in most of the rest of the country, although it does write some insurance in Florida, Georgia, Texas, Illinois, Oklahoma, New York, Virginia, New Jersey and Arizona. In addition to automobile insurance, Mercury writes other lines of insurance in various states, including mechanical breakdown and homeowners insurance.

The Los Angeles-based operation sells policies primarily through independent agents. In all, the company uses about 3,300 independent agents.

Mercury offers bodily injury liability, underinsured and uninsured motorist, personal injury protection, property damage liability, comprehensive, collision and other hazard insurance coverage.

Founded in 1961, Mercury has about 3,800 employees and a market capitalization of about $2.8 billion.

Dividend Yield ☆
2.9 percent (2004)

Dividend Growth (past five years) ☆ ☆ ☆
89 percent

Consistency ☆ ☆ ☆ ☆
Increased dividends more than 15 consecutive years.

Financial Strength
Increased earnings per share only one of the past five years.
Increased assets five of the past five years.

Financial Summary
Fiscal year ended: Dec. 31

	1998	1999	2000	2001	2002	2003	5-Year Growth (%)
Dividends/share ($)	.70	.84	.96	1.06	1.20	1.32	89
Earnings/share ($)	3.22	2.44	2.02	1.94	1.21	3.38	1
Assets ($billions)	1.87	1.91	2.14	2.32	2.65	3.12	67
Dividend yield (%)	1.4	2.6	3.4	2.8	2.7	3.1	—

5-year stock growth (mid-1999 to mid-2004): 70 percent ($30 to $51)

RPM International, Inc.

68

2628 Pearl Road
P.O. Box 777
Medina, Ohio 44258
330.273.5090

NYSE: RPM
www.rpminc.com

Chairman: Thomas C. Sullivan
President and CEO: Frank C. Sullivan

Current Yield	3.7%	
Back-to-the-Future Yield	5-year 4.2%	10-year 5.0%

Rating

Dividend Yield	☆ ☆
Dividend Growth	
Consistency	☆ ☆ ☆ ☆
Financial Strength	☆ ☆
Total	8 points

RPM'S COATINGS COVER HUNDREDS OF BRIDGES, BUILDINGS, SHIPS, AND highways the world over—including the Statue of Liberty and the Eiffel tower. RPM has 68 manufacturing plants in 17 countries, and it markets its products in 130 countries.

The Medina, Ohio, operation divides its business into two primary segments:

Consumer products (45 percent). The company sells the majority of its consumer products in North America. Most of those products are geared to do-it-yourself home improvement consumers. Products include coatings and related products, such as Rust-Oleum and Stops-Rust rust-preventative coatings, and decorative coatings marketed under the brands of Painter's Touch, American Accents and others; the Zinsser family of primer-sealers, including B-I-N, Bulls Eye 1-2-3, Perma-White Mildew Proof Paint and Cover-Stain. Other RPM consumer products include Zinsser's wallcovering preparation and removal products; Bondex and Plastic Wood patch and repair products; Wolman deck coatings, sealants and brighteners; Thibaut wallcoverings; Bondo and Marson auto repair compounds and Mar-Hyde auto body paints and specialty products for the automotive aftermarket. Other products include Varathane, Watco, Mohawk , Guardian and Chemical Coatings woodworking and wood finishing products; the Testors and Floquil brands of model kits, coatings and accessories for the hobbyist market; Pettit, Woolsey and Z-Spar marine coatings; and DAP caulks and sealants.

Industrial products (55 percent of total revenue). The company produces a wide range of waterproofing products, including Tremco roofing systems, Alumanation roofing coatings, Paraseal membranes and Vulkem, Dymeric and Monile sealants. It is also a leader in corrosion protection coatings, which are sold under the brand names of Carboline, Plasite, Mathys, Westfield and TCI. It also makes Dryvit exterior insulation finishing systems; Stonhard and Duracon industrial and commercial floor coatings; and specialized industrial products including Day-Glo fluorescent colorants and pigments; Wolman industrial lumber treatments; Fibergrate and Chemgrate fiberglass reinforced plastic grating; and Euco concrete admixtures.

Founded in 1947, RPM has about 7,900 employees and a market capitalization of about $1.7 billion.

Dividend Yield   ☆ ☆
3.7 percent (2004)

Dividend Growth (past five years)
15 percent

Consistency   ☆ ☆ ☆ ☆
Increased dividends every year since 1947.

Financial Strength   ☆ ☆
Increased earnings per share three of the past five years.
Increased revenues four of the past five years.

Financial Summary
Fiscal year ended: May 31

	1998	1999	2000	2001	2002	2003	5-Year Growth (%)
Dividends/share ($)	.44	.46	.49	.50	.51	.52	18
Earnings/share ($)	.84	.88	.73	.62	.97	1.06	26
Revenue ($billions)	1.62	1.71	1.95	2.01	1.97	2.08	28
Dividend yield (%)	2.7	3.1	4.2	5.4	3.8	3.9	—

5-year stock growth (late-1999 to late-2004): 42 percent ($12 to $17)

Quaker Chemical Corp.

One Quaker Park
901 Hector St.
Conshohocken, PA 19428
610-832-4000

NYSE: KWR
www.quakerchem.com

Chairman and CEO: Ronald J. Naples

Current Yield	3.4%	
Back-to-the-Future Yield	5-year 5.3%	10-year 4.9%

Rating

Dividend Yield	☆ ☆
Dividend Growth	
Consistency	☆ ☆ ☆ ☆
Financial Strength	☆ ☆
Total	8 points

QUAKER CHEMICAL PRODUCES AND SELLS A WIDE RANGE OF CHEMICAL products to industrial customers throughout the world. International sales account for about 55 percent of Quaker's annual revenue.

The Conshohocke, Pennsylvania, operation offers products and services in several different industry segments, including:

Rolling lubricants (23 percent of revenues). Rolling lubricants are used by manufacturers of steel in the hot and cold rolling of steel and by manufacturers of aluminum in the hot rolling of aluminum

Corrosion preventives (9 percent) These products are used by steel and metalworking customers to protect metal during manufacture, storage, and shipment.

Machining and grinding compounds (14 percent). These are used by metalworking customers in cutting, shaping, and grinding metal parts which require special treatment to enable them to tolerate the manufacturing process.

Hydraulic fluids (11 percent). Quaker makes hydraulic fluids used by steel, metalworking, and other customers to operate hydraulically activated equipment.

Chemical management services (11 percent)

Other segments (32 percent). Quaker's other leading business segments include metal finishing compounds (used to prepare metal surfaces for special treatments such as galvanizing and tin plating and to prepare metal for further processing); forming compounds (used to facilitate the drawing and extrusion of metal products); technology for the removal of hydrogen sulfide in various industrial application; chemical milling products for the aerospace industry and temporary and permanent coatings for metal and concrete products; and construction products such as flexible sealants and protective coatings for various applications.

Founded in 1930, Quaker Chemical Corp. has about 1,140 employees and a market capitalization of about $250 million.

Dividend Yield ☆ ☆
3.4 percent (2004)

Dividend Growth (past five years)
15 percent

Consistency ☆ ☆ ☆ ☆
Increased dividends 14 of the past 15 years.

Financial Strength ☆ ☆
Increased earnings per share four of the past five years (but actually declined in earnings by a penny per share during that five-year period). Increased revenues four of the past five years.

Financial Summary
Fiscal year ended: Dec. 31

	1998	1999	2000	2001	2002	2003	5-Year Growth (%)
Dividends/share ($)	.73	.77	.79	.82	.84	.84	15
Earnings/share ($)	1.53	1.74	1.94	.84	1.51	1.52	—
Revenue ($millions)	257	259	268	251	275	340	32
Dividend yield (%)	1.7	2.0	1.9	2.3	2.2	2.6	—

5-year stock growth (late-1999 to late-2004): 38 percent ($16 to $22)

Avery Dennison

150 N. Orange Grove Blvd.
Pasadena, CA 91103
626-304-2000

NYSE: AVY
www.averydennison.com

Chairman and CEO: Philip M. Neal
President: Dean A. Scarborough

Current Yield	2.3%	
Back-to-the-Future Yield	5-year 2.6%	10-year 9.5%

Rating

Dividend Yield	
Dividend Growth	☆ ☆
Consistency	☆ ☆ ☆ ☆
Financial Strength	☆ ☆
Total	8 points

NEED A LABEL? AVERY DENNISON HAS YOU COVERED. AVERY HAS BECOME nearly synonymous with adhesive labels of all types. It is a global leader of self-adhesive materials, labels, tapes, office products and specialty chemical adhesives.

The Pasadena, California, company has operations in 44 countries and markets its products in about 89 countries. International sales account for about 52 percent of Avery's $2.65 billion in annual revenue.

The company has two primary business segments:

Pressure-sensitive products (61 percent of sales) Avery sells Fasson, JAC and Avery Dennison brand pressure-sensitive base materials, specialty tapes, graphic films, reflective highway safety products, and performance polymers. Its base materials consist primarily of papers, plastic films, metal foils and fabrics, which are primed and coated with adhesives, and then laminated with specially coated backing papers and films.

Consumer and converted products (39 percent) The company sells a broad range of products for the home, school and office. Those products include labels for copiers and printers, related computer software, presentation and organizing systems, ink-jet and laser printer card and index products, data-processing labels, binder and presentation dividers, three-ring binders, sheet protectors, and various vinyl and heat-sealed products. It also sells a wide range of other stationery products, including writing instruments, markers, adhesives and specialty products under brand names such as Avery, Stabilo, Marks-A-Lot, HI-LITER and Index Maker. The firm also manufactures and sells a wide range of custom label products, high performance specialty films and labels, automotive products, and tickets, tags, labels and fasteners for the retail apparel industry.

Founded, in 1935, Avery Dennison has about 20,500 employees and a market capitalization of $6 billion.

Dividend Yield
2.3 percent (2004)

Dividend Growth (past five years)   ☆ ☆
67 percent

Consistency   ☆ ☆ ☆ ☆
Increased dividends 14 of the past 15 years.

Financial Strength   ☆ ☆
Increased earnings per share three of the past five years.
Increased revenues four of the past five years.

Financial Summary
Fiscal year ended: Dec. 31

	1998	1999	2000	2001	2002	2003	5-Year Growth (%)
Dividends/share ($)	.87	1.13	1.11	1.23	1.35	1.45	67
Earnings/share ($)	2.15	2.13	2.84	2.47	2.59	2.65	23
Revenue ($billions)	3.5	3.8	3.9	3.8	4.2	4.8	37
Dividend yield (%)	1.7	2.0	1.9	2.3	2.2	2.6	—

5-year stock growth (late-1999 to late-2004): 0 percent ($61 to $61)

ABM Industries

71

160 Pacific Avenue, Suite 222
San Francisco, CA 94111
415-733-4000

NYSE: ABM
www.abm.com

Chairman: Martinn H. Mandles
President and CEO: Henrik C. Slipsager

Current Yield	2.2%	
Back-to-the-Future Yield	5-year 2.8%	10-year 7.6%

Rating

Dividend Yield	
Dividend Growth	☆ ☆
Consistency	☆ ☆ ☆ ☆
Financial Strength	☆ ☆
Total	8 points

ABM INDUSTRIES DOESN'T MIND GETTING A LITTLE GRIT UNDER ITS NAILS. In fact, the San Francisco operation does the dirty work of thousands of corporations and institutions. The company is one of the largest facility services contractors in North America. About half its revenues are generated outside the United States—primarily in Canada.

Building maintenance is ABM's biggest area, providing janitorial and related services for companies in about 40 states. The company offers a wide range of basic cleaning services for a variety of facilities and clients, including office buildings, department stores, theaters, warehouses, educational and medical institutions, and airport terminals.

ABM also has several other key divisions, including:

Engineering Services. The firm provides on-site operating engineers, who control, monitor and maintain all air conditioning, electrical, energy, heating, mechanical, plumbing and ventilation systems at commercial buildings, hotels, schools, factories and warehouses.

Commercial security services. ABM provides security professionals for high-rise buildings, high-tech computer campuses and complexes, financial institutions, data center facilities, and commercial and industrial sites. In all, the security services division has about 11,000 employees in 38 states through 54 branch and district offices.

Parking. ABM manages parking facilities that are either leased from or managed for third parties. Its Ampco System Parking subsidiary operates about 1,700 parking lots and garages in 25 states.

Lighting service. The company provides bulb replacement, fixture cleaning and lighting system maintenance as well as the design, installation and repair of outdoor signs.

Mechanical services. ABM provides heating, ventilation and air conditioning maintenance for commercial and industrial facilities in California and Arizona.

ABM was founded in 1909 in San Francisco as a one-man window cleaning service. The company has about 70,000 employees and a market capitalization of about $925 million.

Dividend Yield
2.2 percent (2004)

Dividend Growth (past five years) ☆ ☆
58 percent

Consistency ☆ ☆ ☆ ☆
Increased dividends more than 15 consecutive years.

Financial Strength ☆ ☆
Increased earnings per share three of the past five years.
Increased revenues more than 15 consecutive years.

Financial Summary
Fiscal year ended: Dec. 31

	1998	1999	2000	2001	2002	2003	5-Year Growth (%)
Dividends/share ($)	.24	.28	.30	.33	.36	.38	58
Earnings/share ($)	.72	.83	.93	.90	.92	.73	1
Revenue ($billions)	1.50	1.63	1.81	1.95	2.19	2.26	51
Dividend yield (%)	1.6	1.9	2.5	2.1	2.2	2.5	—

5-year stock growth (mid-1999 to mid-2004): 50 percent ($12 to $18)

Kimberly-Clark Corp.

72

P.O. Box 619100
Dallas, TX 75261
972-281-1200

NYSE: KMB
www.kimberly-clark.com

President and CEO: Thomas J. Falk

Current Yield	2.4%	
Back-to-the-Future Yield	5-year 2.6%	10-year 5.5%

Rating

Dividend Yield	
Dividend Growth	☆
Consistency	☆ ☆ ☆ ☆
Financial Strength	☆ ☆ ☆
Total	8 points

FROM THE DAY THEY'RE BORN, MANY AMERICANS BECOME INTIMATELY familiar with Kimberly-Clark. The Dallas-based operation is the maker of Huggies diapers—as well as a vast array of other personal products, such as Kleenex and Kotex, that have become an important part of daily life in America.

But the company's reach goes far beyond the U.S. Every day around the world, one out of four people use a Kimberly-Clark product. About 19 percent of its sales are generated in Europe, 60 percent are in North America, and the remaining 21 percent are in Asia, Latin America and other parts of the world.

The company breaks its operations into three key segments:

Personal care (36 percent of sales). The company makes disposable diapers, training and youth pants and swim pants, and feminine and incontinence care products. Leading brands include Huggies, Pull-Ups, Little Swimmers, GoodNites, Kotex, Lightdays, and Depend.

Consumer tissue (38 percent). The firm makes facial and bathroom tissue, paper towels, napkins, wet wipes and related products. Leading brands include Kleenex, Scott, Cottonelle, Viva, Andrex, Scottex, Hakle, and Page.

Business to business (26 percent). Kimberly-Clark makes a variety of products for business and commercial use, including facial and bathroom tissue, paper towels, wipers and napkins. It also makes health care products such as surgical gowns, drapes, infection control products, sterilization wraps, disposable face masks and exam gloves, respiratory products and other disposable medical products. And it makes business and correspondence papers, specialty and technical papers and related products.

Founded in 1872, Kimberly-Clark has about 62,000 employees and a market capitalization of about $33 billion.

Dividend Yield
2.4 percent (2004)

Dividend Growth (past five years)   ☆
37 percent

Consistency   ☆ ☆ ☆ ☆
Increased dividends more than 15 consecutive years.

Financial Strength   ☆ ☆ ☆
Increased earnings per share four of the past five years.
Increased revenues four of the past five years.

Financial Summary
Fiscal year ended: Dec. 31

	1998	1999	2000	2001	2002	2003	5-Year Growth (%)
Dividends/share ($)	.99	1.03	1.08	1.12	1.20	1.36	37
Earnings/share ($)	2.45	2.98	3.31	3.27	3.36	3.38	38
Revenue ($billions)	12.3	13.0	14.0	13.3	13.6	14.3	16
Dividend yield (%)	2.0	1.8	1.8	1.8	2.0	2.7	—

5-year stock growth (mid-1999 to mid-2004): 14 percent ($58 to $66)

ChevronTexaco Corp.

73

575 Market Street
San Francisco, CA 94105
925-842-1000

NYSE: CVX
www.chevrontexaco.com

Chairman and CEO: David J. O'Reily

Current Yield	3.2%	
Back-to-the-Future Yield	5-year 3.3%	10-year 6.6%

Rating

Dividend Yield	☆ ☆
Dividend Growth	
Consistency	☆ ☆ ☆ ☆
Financial Strength	☆ ☆
Total	8 points

CHEVRONTEXACO WAS FORMED THROUGH A 2001 MERGER OF TWO OF THE nation's largest oil companies. The combined company is the nation's second largest energy company. It is also the world's fourth largest publicly-traded firm based on oil-equivalent reserves and fifth largest based on production.

ChevronTexaco owns about 4,000 service stations in the U.S., and supplies gasoline for more than 11,000 other stations.

The company also has operations in about 180 countries around the world.

ChevronTexaco operates on several different fronts in the energy industry, including:

Exploration and production. The company explores for and produces crude oil and natural gas in 25 countries.

Refining, marketing and transportation. As one of the nation's largest refiners, ChevronTexaco turns crude oil into gasoline, diesel and aviation fuels, lubricants, asphalt and chemicals. It is the top seller of asphalt nationwide, and leading single-brand marketer of heavy-duty and industrial oils in North America. In Canada, the company is the leading marketer of transportation fuels with 200 outlets in British Columbia. ChevronTexaco is also a 50 percent owner of Caltex, which is involved in refining, and distribution of fuel in 60 countries.

Chemicals. The firm produces plastics and petrochemicals, including styrene and additives for fuel and lubricants. It has plants in the U.S. and four other countries, and sales in more than 80 countries.

Shipping. The company operates one of the world's largest tanker fleets. The tankers are used to ship crude oil and refined products around the world.

ChevronTexaco owns a 26 percent equity interest in the common stock of Dynegy Inc. (Dynegy), an energy merchant engaged in power generation, natural gas liquids processing and marketing, and regulated energy delivery.

ChevronTexaco traces its roots to the Pacific Coast Oil Company opened in Los Angeles in 1879. The company was acquired by John D. Rockefeller's Standard Oil Trust in 1900, and then spun off into Standard Oil Company of California in 1911 as part of the breakup of Rockefeller's operation. The company changed its name to Chevron in 1984.

The company had about 85,000 employees and a market capitalization of about $95 billion.

Dividend Yield ☆ ☆
3.2 percent (2004)

Dividend Growth (past five years)
17 percent

Consistency ☆ ☆ ☆ ☆
Increased dividends more than 15 consecutive years.

Financial Strength ☆ ☆
Increased earnings per share three of the past five years.
Increased revenue four of the past five years.

Financial Summary
Fiscal year ended: Dec. 31

	1998	1999	2000	2001	2002	2003	5-Year Growth (%)
Dividends/share ($)	2.44	2.48	2.60	2.65	2.80	2.86	17
Earnings/share ($)	1.75	3.00	7.21	370	1.07	6.96	298
Revenue ($billions)	71.9	85.7	119.1	106.2	99.0	121.8	69
Dividend yield (%)	3.0	2.8	3.1	3.0	3.5	4.0	—

5-year stock growth (late-1999 to late-2004): 20 percent ($45 to $54)

Emerson Electric Company 74

8000 W. Florissant Ave.
St. Louis, MO 63136
314-553-2000

NYSE: EMR
www.gotoemerson.com

Chairman and CEO: David M. Farr

Current Yield	2.5%	
Back-to-the-Future Yield	5-year 2.6%	10-year 5.2%

Rating

Dividend Yield	☆
Dividend Growth	☆
Consistency	☆ ☆ ☆ ☆
Financial Strength	☆ ☆
Total	8 points

EMERSON ELECTRIC MANUFACTURERS A WIDE RANGE OF MOTORS FOR industrial and heavy commercial applications, industrial automation equipment, gear drives, power distribution equipment and temperature and environmental control systems.

The St. Louis operation divides its operations into five key segments:

Process Controls (24 percent of annual revenue). The company manufactures measurement and analytical instruments, valves, control systems, and factory automation software.

Industrial automation (18 percent). The company makes industrial motors and drives, industrial machinery, fluid control systems, and heating and lighting equipment.

Electronics and telecommunications (17 percent). Emerson manufactures power supplies, power conditioning equipment, environmental control systems, site monitoring systems, and electrical switching equipment.

Heating, ventilating and air conditioning (18 percent). The firm makes compressors, hermetic terminals, thermostats and valves.

Appliance and tools (24 percent). The company makes hand tools, plumbing and bench power tools, disposals, motors and controls.

Emerson sells its products worldwide, with operations in more than 150 countries. About 45 percent of its revenue comes from foreign sales.

The company was founded in 1890 by John Wesley Emerson shortly after Thomas A. Edison installed his first electrical generators. In his small St. Louis shop, Emerson manufactured room fans, ceiling fans and electrical motors.

Emerson Electric has about 107,000 employees and a market capitalization of about $26 billion.

Dividend Yield ☆
2.5 percent (2004)

Dividend Growth (past five years) ☆
33 percent

Consistency ☆ ☆ ☆ ☆
Increased dividends 19 consecutive years.

Financial Strength ☆ ☆
Increased earnings per share three of the past five years.
Increased revenues three of the past five years.

Financial Summary
Fiscal year ended: Dec. 31

	1998	1999	2000	2001	2002	2003	5-Year Growth (%)
Dividends/share ($)	1.18	1.30	1.43	1.53	1.56	1.57	33
Earnings/share ($)	2.77	3.00	3.30	2.40	2.52	2.41	—
Revenue ($billions)	13.4	14.3	15.5	15.5	13.8	14	7
Dividend yield (%)	2.0	2.1	2.5	2.3	2.9	3.1	—

5-year stock growth (mid-1999 to mid-2004): 0 percent ($62 to $62)

Canadian Imperial Bank of Commerce 75

Commerce Court
Toronto, Ontario, Canada M5L 1A2
416-980-2211

NYSE: BCM
TSE: CM.TO
www.cibc.com

Chairman: William Etherington
CEO: John Hunkin

Current Yield	3.7%	
Back-to-the-Future Yield	5-year 5.6%	10-year 12.6%

Rating

Dividend Yield	☆ ☆
Dividend Growth	☆
Consistency	☆ ☆
Financial Strength	☆ ☆
Total	7 points

THE CANADIAN IMPERIAL BANK OF COMMERCE IS ONE OF CANADA'S largest financial institutions, providing banking and financial services for more than nine million customers.

The Toronto-based institution breaks its business into three primary segments:

Retail markets. The company provides financial services and products to personal and small business customers in Canada. These services are offered through the branch network, telephone banking and online banking. The company has a total of 1,100 branch offices, and about 4,400 ATMs—the largest network of money machines in Canada.

Wealth management. The Canadian Imperial Bank's wealth management division provides investment advisory services and investment products for investors in Canada.

World markets. Canadian Imperial is a leading investment bank in North America with niche services in the U.K. and Asia.

Residential mortgages make up about 45 percent of the bank's total loan portfolio, personal and credit card debt accounts for 21 percent, business and government loans make up 22 percent, and repurchase agreements account for 12 percent.

The Canadian Imperial Bank traces its roots to the Canadian Bank of Commerce, which opened in 1837 and the Imperial Bank of Canada, which opened in 1875. The two banks merged in 1961. The company has about 37,000 employees and a market capitalization of about $23 billion (Canadian dollars).

Dividend Yield ☆ ☆
3.7 percent (2004)

Dividend Growth (past five years) ☆
37 percent

Consistency ☆ ☆
Increased dividends eight of the past 10 years.

Financial Strength ☆ ☆
Increased earnings per share four of the past five years.
Increased assets three of the past five years.

Financial Summary

Fiscal year ended: Oct. 31
All figures are Canadian Dollars

	1998	1999	2000	2001	2002	2003	5-Year Growth (%)
Dividends/share ($)	1.20	1.20	1.29	1.44	1.60	1.64	37
Earnings/share ($)	2.56	2.74	3.57	4.62	1.74	4.12	61
Assets ($billions)	281	250	268	287	273	277	—
Dividend yield (%)	2.8	3.4	3.2	2.9	3.2	3.3	—

5-year stock growth (mid-1999 to mid-2004): 28 percent ($39 to $50)

ServiceMaster Company

2300 Warrenville Road
Downers Grove, IL 60515
630-663-2000

NYSE: SVM
www.servicemaster.com

Chairman and CEO: Jonathon Ward

Current Yield	3.6%	
Back-to-the-Future Yield	5-year 2.6%	10-year 5.7%

Rating

Dividend Yield	☆ ☆
Dividend Growth	☆
Consistency	☆ ☆ ☆ ☆
Financial Strength	
Total	7 points

NEED SOMETHING DONE AROUND THE HOUSE? SERVICEMASTER MAY BE ABLE to help. The Downers Grove, Illinois, operation offers a host of services, including lawn care and landscape maintenance, termite and pest control, plumbing, heating and air conditioning maintenance and repair, and appliance maintenance and repair.

ServiceMaster provides its services for about 10.5 million residential and commercial customers throughout the U.S. and in about 45 foreign countries.

The company offers its services through a network of about 5,400 company-owned and franchised service centers and business units, including TruGreen ChemLawn, TruGreen LandCare, Terminix, American Home Shield, American Residential Services, Rescue Rooter, American Mechanical Services, ServiceMaster Clean, Merry Maids, AmeriSpec and Furniture Medic.

ServiceMaster was founded in 1929 as a mothproofing service, and then expanded to carpet cleaning in 1952. Since then, the company has slowly expanded into other services.

ServiceMaster has about 400,000 employees and a market capitalization of about $3.6 billion.

Dividend Yield ☆ ☆
3.6 percent (2004)

Dividend Growth (past five years) ☆
27 percent

Consistency ☆ ☆ ☆ ☆
Increased dividends more than 10 consecutive years.

Financial Strength
Increased earnings per share only two of the past five years.
Increased revenues two of the past five years.

Financial Summary
Fiscal year ended: Dec. 31

	1998	1999	2000	2001	2002	2003	5-Year Growth (%)
Dividends/share ($)	.33	.36	.38	.40	.41	.42	27
Earnings/share ($)	.64	.72	.61	.38	.56	.54	—
Revenue ($billions)	4.72	5.70	5.97	3.60	3.59	3.57	—
Dividend yield (%)	1.6	2.1	3.4	3.5	3.3	4.1	—

5-year stock growth (mid-1999 to mid-2004): -25 percent ($16 to $12)

May Department Stores

611 Olive St.
St. Louis, MO 63101
314-342-6300

NYSE: MAY
www.maycompany.com

Chairman and CEO: Eugene S. Kahn
President: John L. Dunham

Current Yield	3.8%	
Back-to-the-Future Yield	5-year 2.6%	10-year 2.4%

Rating

Dividend Yield	☆ ☆
Dividend Growth	
Consistency	☆ ☆ ☆ ☆
Financial Strength	☆
Total	7 points

WITH ITS RECENT ACQUISITION OF MARSHAL FIELD'S, MAY NOW HAS ABOUT 482 department stores from coast to coast. It also operates 220 David's Bridal stores, 454 After Hours Formalwear stores, and 10 Priscilla of Boston stores.

May has stores in 46 states, Washington, D.C., and Puerto Rico, although only a few actually carry the May name.

The company breaks its chain store operations down by city headquarters. New York-based Lord & Taylor's has 54 stores; Boston-based Filene's and Kaufmann's have a combined 101 stores; and Houston-based Foley's has 69 stores. Robinson-May and Meier & Frank are both based in Los Angeles, and have a total of 73 stores in six Western states; Hecht's and Strawbridge's are both based in Washington, D.C. and have a total of 81 stores in the seven

Eastern states; and Minneapolis-based Marshall Field's has 62 stores in eight Midwestern states.

The St. Louis-based retailer also has three chains based in St. Louis, including Famous-Barr, L. S. Ayres and The Jones Store, with a total of 42 stores in five Midwestern states.

Founded in 1877, May has about 110,000 employees and a market capitalization of about $7.5 billion.

Dividend Yield ☆ ☆
3.8 percent (2004)

Dividend Growth (past five years)
13 percent

Consistency ☆ ☆ ☆ ☆
Increased dividends 29 consecutive years.

Financial Strength ☆
Increased earnings per share three of the past five years.
Increased revenues two of the past five years.

Financial Summary
Fiscal year ended: Dec. 31

	1998	1999	2000	2001	2002	2003	5-Year Growth (%)
Dividends/share ($)	.85	.90	.93	.94	.95	.96	13
Earnings/share ($)	2.30	2.60	2.62	2.22	2.02	2.08	—
Revenue ($billions)	13.1	13.6	14.2	13.9	13.5	13.3	1
Dividend yield (%)	2.1	2.4	3.4	2.7	3.2	3.9	—

5-year stock growth (mid-1999 to mid-2004): -36 percent ($39 to $25)

R. R. Donnelley & Sons Co.

77 W. Wacker Dr.
Chicago, IL 60601
312-326-8000

NYSE: RRD
www.rrdonnelley.com

Chairman: Stephen M. Wolf
CEO, and President: Mark A. Angelson

Current Yield	3.5%	
Back-to-the-Future Yield	5-year 3.1%	10-year 3.4%

Rating

Dividend Yield	☆ ☆
Dividend Growth	☆
Consistency	☆ ☆ ☆ ☆
Financial Strength	
Total	7 points

R. R. DONNELLEY IS THE LARGEST PRINTING COMPANY IN NORTH AMERICA. But its reach extends far beyond these shores. The Chicago-based operation has more than 600 locations worldwide, with plants in South America, Europe and China.

The company provides a broad range of commercial printing services, including forms and labels, direct mail, financial printing, print fulfillment, business communication outsourcing, logistics, online services, digital photography, and content and database management.

Each year the company publishes thousands of books, magazines, catalogs and directories. Donnelley breaks its business into five key categories:

Magazines, catalogs and inserts (33 percent of annual sales). The company is the leading printer of magazines and catalogs in North

America. It prints the most of the top 10 magazine titles and most of the largest consumer catalogs in North America.

Logistics services (16 percent). Donnelley processes over 20 billion print and mail pieces and over 180 million packages each year.

Books (15 percent). The company is the leading book printer in North America, printing more than half of the *The New York Times'* adult best-seller titles and about a third of all textbooks used in U.S. classrooms.

Telecommunications (14 percent). Donnelley prints the directories for some of the world's largest telephone companies, including SBC, Verizon and Qwest. It also prints directories for independent publishers such as Yellow Book, Feist, RH Donnelley and White Directories, and leading international directory publishers such as Yell and Shanghai Telephone.

Financial (9 percent). Donnelley does a high volume of printing for investment management, banking, insurance, and managed care companies.

Other (13 percent). The company is involved in a wide range of other printing, distribution, and digital photography services.

Founded in 1864, Donnelley has about 50,000 employees and a market capitalization of about $6.5 billion.

Dividend Yield   ☆ ☆
3.5 percent (2004)

Dividend Growth (past five years)   ☆
24 percent

Consistency   ☆ ☆ ☆ ☆
Increased dividends more than 15 consecutive years.

Financial Strength
Increased earnings per share only one of the past five years.
Increased revenues two of the past five years.

Financial Summary
Fiscal year ended: Dec. 31

	1998	1999	2000	2001	2002	2003	5-Year Growth (%)
Dividends/share ($)	.82	.86	.90	.94	.98	1.02	24
Earnings/share ($)	1.93	2.20	2.11	1.47	1.45	1.29	—
Revenue ($billions)	5.02	5.18	5.76	5.30	4.75	4.79	—
Dividend yield (%)	2.0	2.7	3.9	3.3	3.7	4.3	—

5-year stock growth (mid-1999 to mid-2004): 0 percent ($31 to $31)

Bandag, Inc.

2905 N. Hwy. 61
Muscatine, IA 52761
563-262-1400

NYSE: BDG
www.bandag.com

Chairman, CEO, and President: Martin G. Carver

Current Yield	3.1%	
Back-to-the-Future Yield	5-year 4.0%	10-year 2.3%

Rating

Dividend Yield	☆ ☆
Dividend Growth	
Consistency	☆ ☆ ☆ ☆
Financial Strength	☆
Total	7 points

BANDAG IS A WORLD LEADER IN THE MANUFACTURE OF RETREAD TIRES. MOST of its retreads are for large trucks, although it also does retreads for buses, industrial equipment and off road vehicles.

The so-called "Bandag Method" of retreading, which the company promotes as a superior alternative to the traditional "cold-bonding" retreat process, was introduced by Bandag in 1957. The Bandag Method separates the process of vulcanizing the tread rubber from the process of bonding the tread rubber to the tire casing, allowing for optimal temperature and pressure levels at each stage of the retreading process.

The Muscatine, Iowa, operation has about 1,100 franchisees worldwide. Two-thirds of its franchises are located outside the U.S.

Most Bandag franchisees are independent operators of full service tire distributorships. The rest are operated by the company's Tire Distribution Systems division.

The company has rubber production facilities in eight countries.

Bandag has about 3,000 employees and a market capitalization of about $825 million.

Dividend Yield ☆ ☆

3.1 percent (2004)

Dividend Growth (past five years)

16 percent

Consistency ☆ ☆ ☆ ☆

Increased dividends more than 15 consecutive years.

Financial Strength

Increased earnings per share four of the past five years.
Increased *decreased* each of the past five years.

Financial Summary

Fiscal year ended: Dec. 31

	1998	1999	2000	2001	2002	2003	5-Year Growth (%)
Dividends/share ($)	1.11	1.15	1.19	1.23	1.27	1.29	16
Earnings/share ($)	2.63	2.75	2.90	2.12	2.52	3.11	18
Revenue ($billions)	1.06	1.01	.996	.949	.901	.816	—
Dividend yield (%)	2.5	3.6	4.1	4.0	3.6	3.6	—

5-year stock growth (mid-1999 to mid-2004): 25 percent ($36 to $45)

PPG Industries, Inc. **80**

One PPG Place
Pittsburgh, PA 15272
412-434-3131

NYSE: PPG
www.ppg.com

Chairman and CEO: Raymond W. LeBoeuf

Current Yield	3.1%	
Back-to-the-Future Yield	5-year 3.0%	10-year 4.6%

Rating

Dividend Yield	☆ ☆
Dividend Growth	☆
Consistency	☆ ☆ ☆ ☆
Financial Strength	
Total	7 points

PPG INDUSTRIES MAKES A VARIETY OF COATINGS, GLASS, FIBER GLASS AND specialty chemicals for a wide range of industrial applications.

The Pittsburgh operation has operations around the world, with foreign sales accounting for about 43 percent of total revenue. In all, the company has 103 manufacturing facilities in 21 countries.

PPG makes products for a variety of applications, including:

Aerospace. It makes sealants and coatings for commercial and military aircraft.

Architectural coatings. Its leading brands include Olympic, Pittsburgh Paints, Lucite and Monarch.

Automotive coatings.

Automotive glass. The company makes automotive window glass for both the original manufacturing and replacement glass business.

Fiberglass. PPG makes fiberglass primarily for circuit boards, specialty materials and as a reinforcing agent.

Fine chemicals. PPG makes intermediaries and ingredients for the pharmaceutical industry.

Flat Glass

Industrial coatings

Optical products

Packaging coatings.

Founded in 1883, PPG has about 31,000 employees and a market capitalization of about $9.8 billion.

Dividend Yield ☆ ☆
3.1 percent (2004)

Dividend Growth (past five years) ☆
22 percent

Consistency ☆ ☆ ☆ ☆
Increased dividends for 33 consecutive years.

Financial Strength
Increased earnings per share only one of the past five years.
Increased revenues three of the past five years.

Financial Summary
Fiscal year ended: Dec. 31

	1998	1999	2000	2001	2002	2003	5-Year Growth (%)
Dividends/share ($)	1.42	1.52	1.60	1.68	1.71	1.73	2
Earnings/share ($)	4.13	3.68	3.79	2.29	-.41	2.89	—
Revenue ($billions)	7.51	7.76	8.63	8.17	8.07	8.76	17
Dividend yield (%)	2.3	2.6	3.4	3.3	3.3	3.3	—

5-year stock growth (mid-1999 to mid-2004): -5 percent ($62 to $59)

BellSouth Corp.

81

1155 Peachtree St., N.E.
Atlanta, GA 30309
404-249-2000

NYSE: BLS
www.bellsouth.com

Chairman, president and CEO: F. Duane Ackerman

Current Yield	4.0%	
Back-to-the-Future Yield	5-year 2.1%	10-year 6.7%

Rating

Dividend Yield	☆ ☆ ☆
Dividend Growth	☆
Consistency	
Financial Strength	☆ ☆
Total	6 points

BELLSOUTH IS ONE OF THE BABY BELL REGIONAL PHONE COMPANIES. IN ALL, the company serves more than 45 million local, long distance, Internet and wireless customers in the U.S and 13 other countries.

The company offers voice, broadband data and e-commerce services to business customers, and basic phone and related services and high-speed internet service to residential customers.

The Atlanta operation also owns a 40 percent stake in Cingular Wireless.

BellSouth has a couple of key subsidiaries, including BellSouth Telecommunications, Inc. (BST), which offers standard phone and Internet services in the southeastern U.S., including Alabama, Florida, Georgia, Kentucky, Louisiana, Mississippi, North Carolina, South Carolina and Tennessee. It also operates BellSouth Long Distance (BSLD), which offers long distance services in those nine states. In all, the company has about 16 million retail and wholesale customers in its primary service area.

The company's communications group accounts for most of its total revenue.

The balance comes from its Latin American and international operations.

BellSouth was incorporated and made its initial public stock offering in 1983 as part of the break up of the Bell System. The company has 75,745 employees and a market capitalization of about $47 billion.

Dividend Yield
4.0 percent (2004)

Dividend Growth (past five years)
26 percent

Consistency
Increased dividends only five of the past 10 years.

Financial Strength
Increased earnings per share three of the past five years.
Increased revenues three of the past five years.

Financial Summary
Fiscal year ended: Dec. 31

	1998	1999	2000	2001	2002	2003	5-Year Growth (%)
Dividends/share ($)	.73	.76	.76	.76	.79	.92	26
Earnings/share ($)	1.65	1.98	2.18	2.10	1.13	2.07	25
Revenue ($billions)	23.1	25.2	26.2	24.1	22.4	22.6	—
Dividend yield (%)	2.1	1.7	1.7	1.9	2.6	3.7	—

5-year stock growth (mid-1999 to mid-2004): -40 percent ($45 to $27)

Energy East Corp.

P.O. Box 12904
Albany, NY 12212
518-434-3049

NYSE: EAS
www.energyeast.com

Chairman, CEO, and President: Wesley W. von Schack

Current Yield	4.6%	
Back-to-the-Future Yield	5-year 4.1%	10-year 8.4%

Rating

Dividend Yield	☆ ☆ ☆
Dividend Growth	☆
Consistency	☆ ☆
Financial Strength	
Total	6 points

ENERGY EAST IS AN ALBANY, NEW YORK, UTILITY THAT SERVES NEARLY 3 million customers. The company provides both electricity and natural gas for residents in New York, Maine, Massachusetts, Connecticut, and New Hampshire.

About 60 percent of its business involves electric service, 31 percent involves natural gas, and the other 9 percent comes from related areas of the energy business.

The company does business through several subsidiaries, including:

Berkshire Gas, which delivers natural gas to 35,000 customers in western Massachusetts;

Central Maine Power, which delivers electricity to 564,000 customers in central and southern Maine

Connecticut Natural Gas, which provides gas to 147,000 customers in central Connecticut;

NYSEG, which delivers electricity to 838,000 customers and natural gas to 250,000 across upstate New York;

Rochester Gas & Electric, which provides electricity and natural gas energy and related services to approximately 650,000 residents and businesses in a nine-county region centering around the City of Rochester in Upstate New York;

Southern Connecticut Gas, which delivers natural gas to 167,000 customers in southern Connecticut.

Energy East has about 6,300 employees and a market capitalization of about $3.3 billion.

Dividend Yield ☆ ☆ ☆
4.5 percent (2004)

Dividend Growth (past five years) ☆
28 percent

Consistency ☆ ☆
Increased dividends six consecutive years.

Financial Strength
Increased earnings per share only two of the past five years.
Increased revenues four of the past five years.

Financial Summary
Fiscal year ended: Dec. 31

	1998	1999	2000	2001	2002	2003	5-Year Growth (%)
Dividends/share ($)	.78	.84	.88	.92	.96	1.00	28
Earnings/share ($)	1.51	1.91	2.07	2.00	1.50	1.43	—
Revenue ($billions)	2.5	2.3	3.0	3.8	4.0	4.6	84
Dividend yield (%)	3.5	3.3	4.2	4.7	4.6	4.8	—

5-year stock growth (mid-1999 to mid-2004): -6 percent ($26 to $24.50)

Ameren Corp.

19011 Chouteau St.
St. Louis, MO 63166
314-621-3222

NYSE: AEE
www.ameren.com

Chairman, CEO, and President: Gary L. Rainwater

Current Yield	5.6%	
Back-to-the-Future Yield	5-year 6.8%	10-year 7.3%

Rating

Dividend Yield	☆ ☆ ☆ ☆
Dividend Growth	
Consistency	
Financial Strength	☆ ☆
Total	6 points

AMEREN IS A DIVERSIFIED UTILITY COMPANY IN ILLINOIS AND MISSOURI, providing electricity to about 1.7 million residents and natural gas to about 500,000 customers.

The St. Louis operation breaks its business into four key subsidiaries:

UE. Also known as Union Electric Company, UE generates and transmits electricity and distributes natural gas in Missouri and Illinois.

CIPS. Also known as Central Illinois Public Service Company, it supplies electricity and natural gas in Illinois.

Genco. Also known as Ameren Energy Generating Company, the firm operates a non rate-regulated electric generation business.

CILCO. Also known as Central Illinois Light Company, it operates a regulated electric transmission and distribution business, a primarily non rate-regulated electric generation business and a regulated natural gas distribution business in Illinois.

Formed in 1997 with merger of Union Electric and Central Illinois Public Service, Ameren has about 7,650 employees and a market capitalization of about $8 billion

Dividend Yield ☆ ☆ ☆ ☆
5.6 percent (2004)

Dividend Growth (past five years)
0%

Consistency
Has not increased dividends since 1997.

Financial Strength ☆ ☆
Increased earnings per share three of the past five years.
Increased revenues four of the past five years.

Financial Summary
Fiscal year ended: Dec. 31

	1998	1999	2000	2001	2002	2003	5-Year Growth Total (%)
Dividends/share ($)	2.54	2.54	2.54	2.54	2.54	2.54	—
Earnings/share ($)	2.82	2.81	3.33	3.41	2.66	3.14	11
Revenue ($billions)	33.2	35.2	38.6	45.1	38.4	45.9	38
Dividend yield (%)	6.3	6.7	6.9	6.2	6.1	6.0	—

5-year stock growth (mid-1999 to mid-2004): 15 percent ($39 to $45)

Great Plains Energy, Inc.

84

1201 Walnut St.
Kansas City, MO 64106
816-556-2200

NYSE: GXP
www.greatplainsenergy.com

Chairman and CEO: Michael J. Chesser
President: William H. Downey

Current Yield	5.4%	
Back-to-the-Future Yield	5-year 6.6%	10-year 7.8%

Rating

Dividend Yield	☆ ☆ ☆ ☆
Dividend Growth	
Consistency	
Financial Strength	☆ ☆
Total	6 points

GREAT PLAINS ENERGY IS THE PARENT COMPANY OF KANSAS CITY POWER & Light. The utility serves nearly half a million customers in 24 northwestern Missouri and Kansas counties.

The Kansas City, Missouri operation owns six power plants with 21 generating units to provide power to its own customers as well as the wholesale market. In all, the company has 4,100 megawatts of generating capacity. Great Plains is among the most cost efficient utilities in the country, in part, because it uses lower cost coal to provide about 75 percent of its power generation.

Great Plains is also the parent company of Strategic Energy, a Pittsburgh-based supplier of retail electricity in ten states with deregulated energy markets including California, Connecticut, Maryland, Massachusetts, Michigan, New Jersey, New York, Ohio, Pennsylvania and Texas. For a management fee, the company buys wholesale power under long-term contracts for direct delivery to retail customers.

Great Plains Energy was first incorporated in 2001, but its predecessor, Kansas City Power & Light, was founded in 1882. The company has about 2,500 employees and a market capitalization of about $2.1 billion.

Dividend Yield ☆ ☆ ☆ ☆
5.4 percent (2004)

Dividend Growth (past five years)
1 percent

Consistency
Has increased dividends only once in five years.

Financial Strength
Increased earnings per three of the past five years.
Increased revenues four of the past five years.

Financial Summary
Fiscal year ended: Dec. 31

	1998	1999	2000	2001	2002	2003	5-Year Growth (%)
Dividends/share ($)	1.64	1.66	1.66	1.66	1.66	1.66	1
Earnings/share ($)	1.89	1.26	2.05	- .30	1.99	2.07	10
Revenue ($billions)	.94	.92	1.15	1.46	1.86	2.15	—
Dividend yield (%)	5.5	6.6	6.5	6.6	7.3	6.0	—

5-year stock growth (mid-1999 to mid-2004): 20 percent ($25 to $30)

Cinergy Corp.

85

139 E. 4th St.
Cincinnati, OH 45202
800-544-6900

NYSE: CIN
www.cinergy.com

Chairman, CEO, and President: James E. Rogers

Current Yield	4.7 %	
Back-to-the-Future Yield	5-year 6.4%	10-year 7.7%

Rating

Dividend Yield	☆ ☆ ☆	
Dividend Growth		
Consistency		
Financial Strength	☆ ☆ ☆	
Total	6 points	

CINERGY CORP. IS THE PARENT COMPANY OF CINCINNATI GAS & ELECTRIC Company and PSI Energy. The company provides electricity and natural gas in Ohio, Indiana and Kentucky.

PSI, an Indiana corporation organized in 1942, is a vertically integrated and regulated electric utility that provides service in north central, central, and southern Indiana.

The Cincinnati utility also owns Union Light, Heat and Power Company, a Kentucky utility that provides electricity and natural gas service in northern Kentucky.

Cinergy Corp. has a balanced portfolio consisting of two core businesses: regulated operations and commercial businesses. It has 1.5 million electric customers and about 500,000 gas customers. Cinergy's commercial business unit focuses on low-cost electricity generation, owning 6,300 megawatts of capacity.

Cinergy's other subsidiaries (which have little impact on the bottom line) include Cinergy Services, Cinergy Investments, and Cinergy Wholesale Energy.

Cinergy traces its roots to 1837 when the Cincinnati Gas Company was founded. The company has about 7,700 employees and a stock market capitalization of about $7 billion.

Dividend Yield   ☆ ☆ ☆
4.7 percent (2004)

Dividend Growth (past five years)
2 percent

Consistency
Has increased dividends only twice in the past six years.

Financial Strength   ☆ ☆ ☆
Increased earnings per share four of the past five years.
Increased revenues four of the past five years.

Financial Summary
Fiscal year ended: Dec. 31

	1998	1999	2000	2001	2002	2003	5-Year Growth (%)
Dividends/share ($)	1.80	1.80	1.80	1.80	1.80	1.84	2
Earnings/share ($)	1.97	2.10	2.50	2.75	2.13	2.63	34
Revenue ($billions)	3.40	3.43	3.75	3.59	4.06	4.42	30
Dividend yield (%)	5.2	6.1	6.6	5.6	5.4	5.2	—

5-year stock growth (mid-1999 to mid-2004): 38 percent ($29 to $40)

California Water Service Group

1720 N. First St.
San Jose, CA 95112
408-367-8200

NYSE: CWT
www.calwater.com

Chairman: Robert W. Foy
President and CEO: Peter C. Nelson

Current Yield	4.2%	
Back-to-the-Future Yield	5-year 4.2%	10-year 6.4%

Rating

Dividend Yield	☆ ☆ ☆
Dividend Growth	
Consistency	☆ ☆ ☆
Financial Strength	
Total	6 points

IT'S UNLIKELY CALIFORNIA WATER WOULD EVER RUN OUT OF CUSTOMERS—as long as it doesn't run out of water.

The San Jose utility provides water for about 2 million customers in about 100 communities in California, Washington, Hawaii, and New Mexico.

Its biggest customer base is in California, where the company provides water services for about 500,000 residential customers

California Water Service Group is also the parent company of Washington Water Service Company, New Mexico Water Service Company, Hawaii Water Service Company, and CWS Utility Services.

Residential service accounts for about 70 percent of the company's total revenue, business customers make up 18 percent, public authorities, 5 percent, industrial, 4 percent, and other, 3 percent.

Founded in 1926, California Water has about 815 employees and a market capitalization of about $450 million.

Dividend Yield   ☆ ☆ ☆
4.2 percent (2004)

Dividend Growth (past five years)
6 percent

Consistency   ☆ ☆ ☆
Increased dividends nine of the past 10 years.

Financial Strength
Increased earnings per share only two of the past five years.
Increased revenues five consecutive years.

Financial Summary
Fiscal year ended: Dec. 31

	1998	1999	2000	2001	2002	2003	5-Year Growth (%)
Dividends/share ($)	1.07	1.09	1.10	1.12	1.12	1.13	5
Earnings/share ($)	1.31	1.44	1.31	.97	1.25	1.21	—
Revenue ($millions)	186	206	245	247	263	277	49
Dividend yield (%)	4.2	4.0	4.3	4.4	4.5	4.2	—

5-year stock growth (mid-1999 to mid-2004): -10 percent ($30o $27)

Unitrin, Inc.

One East Wacker Dr.
Chicago, IL 60601
312-661-4600

NYSE: UTR
www.unitrin.com

Chairman and CEO: Richard C. Vie
President: Donald G. Southwell

Current Yield	4.0%	
Back-to-the-Future Yield	5-year 4.5%	10-year 7.4%

Rating

Dividend Yield	☆ ☆ ☆
Dividend Growth	☆
Consistency	☆ ☆
Financial Strength	
Total	6 points

UNITRIN SELLS PROPERTY, CASUALTY, LIFE AND HEALTH INSURANCE THROUGH six operating segments, including Multi Lines Insurance, Specialty Lines Insurance, Kemper Auto and Home, Unitrin Direct, Life and Health Insurance and Consumer Finance.

The Chicago-based operation sells automobile, homeowners, commercial multi-peril, motorcycle, boat and watercraft, fire, casualty, workers compensation, and other types of property and casualty insurance to individuals and businesses. Automobile insurance accounts for about 56 percent of the company's premiums.

Multi Lines Insurance, based in Dallas, sells insurance in 30 states. Its leading lines are preferred and standard risk automobile, homeowners, fire, commercial multi-peril and workers compensation insurance. The Multi Lines policies are marketed by more than 1,300 independent insurance agents.

Unitrin's Specialty Lines Insurance division, also based in Dallas, specializes in personal and commercial automobile, motorcycle, and specialty watercraft insurance. Specialty Lines Insurance products account for about 29 percent of the Unitrin's premium revenues.

Unitrin acquired Kemper Auto and Home Insurance Company in 2002. Kemper's auto and home insurance sales account for about 33 percent of Unitrin's premium revenue.

Unitrin has about 8,800 employees and a market capitalization of about $3 billion.

Dividend Yield   ☆ ☆ ☆
4.0 percent (2004)

Dividend Growth (past five years)   ☆
28 percent

Consistency   ☆ ☆
Increased dividends eight of the past 10 years.

Financial Strength
Increased earnings per share only one of the past five years.
Increased revenues five of the past five years.

Financial Summary
Fiscal year ended: Dec. 31

	1998	1999	2000	2001	2002	2003	5-Year Growth (%)
Dividends/share ($)	1.30	1.40	1.50	1.60	1.66	1.66	28
Earnings/share ($)	1.96	1.94	1.60	.75	.01	1.45	—
Revenue ($billions)	1.52	1.70	1.81	1.91	2.30	2.91	91
Dividend yield (%)	3.9	3.9	4.5	4.2	4.7	5.6	—

5-year stock growth (mid-1999 to mid-2004): 24 percent ($33 to $41)

Stanley Works

88

1000 Stanley Dr., Box 7000
New Britain, CT 06050
203-225-5111

NYSE: SWK
www.stanleyworks.com

Chairman and CEO: John F. Lundgren

Current Yield	2.6%	
Back-to-the-Future Yield	5-year 3.6%	10-year 5.2%

Rating

Dividend Yield	☆
Dividend Growth	☆
Consistency	☆ ☆ ☆ ☆
Financial Strength	
Total	6 points

STANLEY WORKS BEGAN OPERATIONS IN 1843 WHEN FREDERICK TRENT Stanley opened a shop in New Britain, Connecticut to manufacture door bolts and other hardware from wrought iron. Now, 161 years later, Stanley's little shop has become a major manufacturer of a broad range of tools and hardware sold around the world.

International sales account for about 31 percent of Stanley's total revenue.

Still based in New Britain, the company separates its operations into two business segments:

Tools. Tool manufacturing is Stanley's primary line of business. It makes carpenters, mechanics, pneumatic and hydraulic tools and tool sets that are sold to customers and distributed directly to retailers. Carpenters tools include hand tools such as measuring instruments, planes, hammers, knives and blades, screwdrivers, saws, chisels, boring tools, masonry, tile and drywall tools, as well as electronic stud sensors, levels, alignment tools and elevation measuring systems. Brands include Stanley, FatMax, MaxGrip, Powerlock, IntelliTools, Dynagrip, and Goldblatt brands. Its mechanics tools include consumer, industrial and professional mechanics hand tools, including wrenches, sockets, electronic diagnostic tools, toolboxes and high-density industrial storage and retrieval systems. Pneumatic tools include fastening tools and fasteners (nails and staples) used for construction, remodeling, furniture making, pallet manufacturing and consumer use and pneumatic air tools.

Doors. The company manufactures automatic doors, as well as closet doors and systems, door locking systems, commercial and consumer hardware, security access control systems and patient monitoring devices. Products include mirrored closet doors and closet organizing systems, automatic doors as well as related door hardware products ranging from hinges, hasps, bolts and latches to shelf brackets and lock sets. Brand names include Stanley, Magic-Door Stanley-Acmetrack, Monarch, Acme, WanderGuard , StanVision and BEST brands.

Stanley Works has about 13,400 employees and a market capitalization of about $3.6 billion.

Dividend Yield   ☆
2.6 percent (2004)

Dividend Growth (past five years)   ☆
25 percent

Consistency   ☆ ☆ ☆ ☆
Increased dividends more than 15 consecutive years.

Financial Strength
Increased earnings per share only two of the past five years.
Increased revenues two of the past five years.

Financial Summary
Fiscal year ended: Dec. 31

	1998	1999	2000	2001	2002	2003	5-Year Growth (%)
Dividends/share ($)	.83	.87	.90	.94	.99	1.04	25
Earnings/share ($)	1.54	1.52	2.22	2.31	2.31	1.90	23
Revenue ($billions)	2.73	2.75	2.75	2.62	2.59	2.68	—
Dividend yield (%)	2.0	3.1	3.5	2.4	2.5	3.6	—

5-year stock growth (mid-1999 to mid-2004): 57 percent ($28 to $44)

V.F. Corp.

89

628 Green Valley Road, Suite 500
Greensboro, NC 27408
336-547-6000

NYSE: VFC
www.vfc.com

Chairman, president and CEO: Mackey J. McDonald

Current Yield	2.2%	
Back-to-the-Future Yield	5-year 2.5%	10-year 4.2%

Rating

Dividend Yield	
Dividend Growth	☆
Consistency	☆ ☆ ☆ ☆
Financial Strength	☆
Total	6 points

V.F. CORP. IS THE WORLD'S LARGEST PUBLICLY-TRADED APPAREL MAKER AND distributor. It sells jeans, intimate apparel, sportswear, and other clothing lines around the world. Foreign sales account for about 21 percent of the company's total sales.

Founded in 1899 as Vanity Fair, .V.F. was a forerunner to Victoria's Secret, producing a wide array of intimate apparel. The Greensboro, North Carolina operation still makes a line of lingerie, sleepwear and intimate apparel under the Vanity Fair brand, but in recent years, silk and satin has taken a back seat to denim and twill.

The company is a leading maker of jeans and denim apparel. Its leading brands include Lee, Wrangler, Rustler, Riders, Brittania, and Earl Jean. V.F. holds about 21 percent share of the U.S. jeans market.

It also makes several other well-known apparel lines, including Nautica sportswear, and JanSport, Eastpak, Kipling, and The North Face outdoor apparel.

The company has 52,000 employees and a market capitalization of about $5.4 billion.

Dividend Yield
2.2 percent (2004)

Dividend Growth (past five years)   ☆
25 percent

Consistency   ☆ ☆ ☆ ☆
Increased dividends more than 15 consecutive years.

Financial Strength   ☆
Increased earnings per share three of the past five years.
Increased revenues three of the past five years.

Financial Summary
Fiscal year ended: Dec. 31

	1998	1999	2000	2001	2002	2003	5-Year Growth (%)
Dividends/share ($)	.81	.85	.89	.94	.97	1.01	25
Earnings/share ($)	3.10	3.05	2.94	2.68	3.38	3.61	16
Revenue ($billions)	5.48	5.55	5.75	5.52	5.08	5.21	—
Dividend yield (%)	2.7	2.4	1.7	2.0	2.3	2.5	—

5-year stock growth (mid-1999 to mid-2004): 28 percent ($36 to $46)

New Plan Excel Realty Trust

1120 Sixth Ave.
New York, NY 10036
212-869-3000

NYSE: NXL
www.newplanexcel.com

Chairman: William Newman
CEO: Glen Rufrano
President: Scott MacDonald

Current Yield	7.2%	
Back-to-the-Future Yield	5-year 8.8%	10-year 7.6%

Rating

Dividend Yield	☆ ☆ ☆ ☆
Dividend Growth	
Consistency	☆
Financial Strength	
Total	5 points

NEW PLAN EXCEL OWNS MORE THAN 350 SHOPPING CENTERS AND OTHER retail properties in 35 states. In all, the New York-based real estate investment trust (REIT) owns more than 50 million square feet of retail space.

Including properties held through joint ventures, New Plan Excel has ownership interests in more than 400 properties. Those properties include 375 community and neighborhood shopping centers, 15 single tenant properties, four enclosed malls and specialized retail centers, and seven other commercial properties.

The company's biggest concentration of shopping centers is in Texas, where it owns 84 properties. The company also owns 30 properties in Florida and 32 in Georgia.

Its biggest tenant is the grocery retailer Kroger, which accounts for about 4 percent of the company's rent base. Other leading tenants include Wal-Mart, 3.5 percent; Kmart, 2.7 percent; Ahold USA, 2.2 percent; and TJX, 1.8 percent.

Founded in 1972, New Plan Excel has about 380 employees and a stock market capitalization of about $2.3 billion.

Dividend Yield   ☆ ☆ ☆ ☆
7.2 percent (2004)

Dividend Growth (past five years)
7 percent

Consistency   ☆
Increased dividends only seven of the past 10 years.

Financial Strength
Increased earnings only one of the past five years.
Increased revenues four of the past five years.

Financial Summary
Fiscal year ended: Dec. 31

	1998	1999	2000	2001	2002	2003	5-Year Growth (%)
Dividends/share ($)	1.49	1.62	1.65	1.65	1.65	1.65	7
Earnings/share ($)	1.50	1.42	1.14	.94	1.13	1.08	—
Revenue ($millions)	205	294	291	294	388	480	134
Dividend yield (%)	7.4	8.7	11.0	9.8	8.6	7.5	—

5-year stock growth (mid-1999 to mid-2004): 26 percent ($19 to $24)

TransCanada Corp.

TransCanada Corp.

TransCanada Corp. 91

TCLP Tower
111 5th Ave. S.W.
Calgary, Alberta, Canada T2P 3Y6
403-267-6100

NYSE: TRP
www.transcanada.com

President and CEO: Harold Kvisle

Current Yield	4.5%	
Back-to-the-Future Yield	5-year 7.2%	10-year 6.1%

Rating

Dividend Yield	☆ ☆ ☆
Dividend Growth	
Consistency	☆
Financial Strength	☆
Total	5 points

TRANSCANADA IS APTLY NAMED. ITS NATURAL GAS PIPELINE CROSSES A LARGE swathe of Canada—particularly Western Canada. Its pipelines span from the Alberta border to Ontario, Quebec and the United States. In all, it has more than 24,000 miles of pipeline, making it the most extensive natural gas pipeline network in Canada.

In addition to its own pipelines, the Calgary operation has interests in several other gas pipeline networks, including Trans Quebec & Maritimes (50 percent stake), Great Lakes (50 Percent), TC PipeLines (33 percent), and Iroquois (41 percent).

The company is also involved in power generation. It owns, controls or is constructing facilities capable of producing more than 4,700 megawatts of power - enough to provide power for about 4.7 million households.

TransCanada has been very aggressive in acquiring other companies and facilities. It acquired Gas Transmission Northwest Corp. in 2004, Foothills Pipelines and Bruce Power in 2003, the ManChief Power Plant in 2002, and the Curtis Palmer hydroelectric plants in 2001.

Founded in 1951, TransCanada has about 2,400 employees and a market capitalization of about $9 billion.

Dividend Yield ☆ ☆ ☆
4.5 percent (2004)

Dividend Growth (past five years)
6 percent

Consistency ☆
Increased dividends seven of the past 10 years.

Financial Strength ☆
Increased earnings per share four of the past five years.
Increased revenues only two of the past five years.

Financial Summary
Fiscal year ended: Dec. 31

	1998	1999	2000	2001	2002	2003	5-Year Growth (%)
Dividends/share ($)	.78	.71	.55	.58	.62	.83	6
Earnings/share ($)	.81	.76	.83	.89	.99	1.28	58
Revenue ($billions)	11.2	8.2	13.8	3.3	3.3	4.1	—
Dividend yield (%)	4.1	5.5	6.5	4.8	4.4	4.5	—

5-year stock growth (late-1999 to late-2004): 83 percent ($12 to $22)

Telecom Corp. of New Zealand (ADS) 92

Telecom Jervois Quay
68 Jervois Quay
P.O. Box 570
Wellington, NZ
800-208-2130

NYSE: NZT
www.telecom.co.nz

Chairman: Roderick Deane
CEO: Theresa Gattung

Current Yield	4.0%	
Back-to-the-Future Yield	5-year 3.0%	10-year 4.5%

Rating

Dividend Yield	☆ ☆ ☆
Dividend Growth	
Consistency	
Financial Strength	☆ ☆
Total	5 points

TELECOM CORPORATION OF NEW ZEALAND IS THE PRIMARY NATIONAL telephone company of New Zealand, but it also offers services in Australia as well. The company's services include voice, mobile and fixed line calling and Internet and data services.

The Wellington-based operation has 1.3 million mobile accounts in New Zealand and 260,000 in Australia. It has about 1.8 million residential and business lines in New Zealand and about 450,000 fixed line customers in Australia.

Telecom has tried to stay on the leading edge of telecommunications technology. Nearly 100 percent of its inter-city trunk routes are fiber optic, and all customer lines are connected to digital exchanges. It offers broadband coverage to about 90 percent of New Zealand households.

Prior to 1987, Telecom New Zealand had been a division of the New Zealand Post Office. The company was spun off in 1987, and went public with its initial stock offering in 1990. The company has about 6,700 employees and a market capitalization of about $7 billion.

Dividend Yield ☆ ☆ ☆
4.0 percent (2004)

Dividend Growth (past five years)
None

Consistency
Increased dividends only four of the last 10 years.

Financial Strength ☆ ☆
Increased earnings per share three of the past five years.
Increased revenues three of the past five years.

Financial Summary
Fiscal year ended: June 30

	1999	2000	2001	2002	2003	2004	5-Year Growth (%)
Dividends/share ($)	2.26	1.80	.65	.78	.93	1.25	—
Earnings/share ($)	1.50	1.56	1.50	1.34	1.87	2.07	38
Revenue ($billions)	2.5	2.87	3.72	3.65	3.42	3.55	42
Dividend yield (%)	6.4	5.4	3.2	4.5	4.7	4	—

5-year stock growth (mid-1999 to mid-2004): -6 percent ($32 to $30)

Entergy Corp.

93

639 Loyola Ave.
New Orleans, LA 70113
504-529-5262

NYSE: ETR
www.entergy.com

Chairman: Robert Luft
CEO: J. Wayne Leonard

Current Yield	3.0 %	
Back-to-the-Future Yield	**5-year 6.3%**	**10-year 6.1%**

Rating

Dividend Yield	☆ ☆
Dividend Growth	
Consistency	☆
Financial Strength	☆ ☆
Total	5 points

ENTERGY SUPPLIES ELECTRICITY TO 2.6 MILLION RESIDENTS OF ARKANSAS, Louisiana, Mississippi, and Texas. The company operates its business through electric subsidiaries in all four sates. It owns and operates power plants with about 30,000 megawatts of electricity.

With annual revenues of more than $9 billion, it is one of the nation's largest utilities. The company serves a wide range of customers, including residential (39 percent of electricity revenues), commercial (28 percent), industrial (30 percent), and other customers (3 percent).

The New Orleans-based utility also operates nuclear power plants in New York, Massachusetts, Vermont, Arkansas, Louisiana, and Mississippi. It is the nation's second largest nuclear generator.

Entergy also operates a commodity service that is a wholesale provider of energy, and operates a network of natural gas pipelines and storage facilities.

Originally incorporated in 1949 Entergy has about 14,800 employees and a market capitalization of about $13 billion.

Dividend Yield   ☆ ☆
3.0 percent (2004)

Dividend Growth (past five years)
7 percent

Consistency   ☆
Has increased dividends four consecutive years.

Financial Strength   ☆ ☆
Increased earnings per five of the past five years.
Increased revenues two of the past five years.

Financial Summary
Fiscal year ended: Dec. 31

	1998	1999	2000	2001	2002	2003	5-Year Growth (%)
Dividends/share ($)	1.50	1.20	1.22	1.28	1.34	1.60	7
Earnings/share ($)	2.22	2.25	2.97	3.08	3.68	3.69	66
Revenue ($billions)	11.5	8.77	10	9.62	8.31	9.2	—
Dividend yield (%)	5.2	4.1	4.1	3.3	3.2	3.1	—

5-year stock growth (mid-1999 to mid-2004): 94 percent ($31 to $60)

Exxon Mobil Corp.

94

5959 Las Colinas Blvd.
Irving, TX 75039

NYSE: XOM
www.exxonmovbile.com

Chairman and CEO: Lee R. Raymond

Current Yield	2.2%	
Back-to-the-Future Yield	5-year 2.7%	10-year 6.6%

Rating

Dividend Yield	
Dividend Growth	☆
Consistency	☆ ☆ ☆ ☆
Financial Strength	
Total	5 points

CREATED THROUGH THE 1999 MERGER OF EXXON AND MOBIL OIL, EXXON Mobil is the world's largest publicly-traded oil company. The firm traces its roots to John D. Rockefeller, who founded the company in 1882 as "Standard Oil."

Exxon Mobil has operations and sales in about 200 countries. Its principal operations include exploration and production of crude oil and natural gas, as well as transportation and retail sales of petroleum products.

In addition to gasoline and oil for automobiles, the company is a major manufacturer and marketer of basic petrochemicals, including olefins, aromatics, polyethylene and polypropylene plastics and a wide variety of specialty products. Exxon Mobil also has interests in electric power generation facilities.

Exxon Mobil produces about 2.5 million barrels of crude oil per day and 10.1 billion cubic feet of natural gas.

The company operates wells and natural gas operations around the world, although North America accounts for the vast majority of its production. The U.S. accounts for about 75 percent of its gross oil production, and Canada accounts for about 14 percent. In gas production, the U.S. accounts for about 56 percent and Canada accounts for about 31 percent.

The company has about 40,000 retail gasoline service stations.

Exxon Mobil has about 88,000 employees and a market capitalization of about $285 billion.

Dividend Yield
2.2 percent (2004)

Dividend Growth (past five years)   ☆
20 percent

Consistency   ☆ ☆ ☆ ☆
Increased dividends more than 15 consecutive years.

Financial Strength
Increased earnings per share two of the past five years.
Increased revenue three of the past five years.

Financial Summary
Fiscal year ended: Dec. 31

	1998	1999	2000	2001	2002	2003	5-Year Growth (%)
Dividends/share ($)	.82	.84	.88	.91	.92	.98	20
Earnings/share ($)	1.14	1.12	2.24	2.17	1.68	3.23	183
Revenue ($billions)	165	182	228	209	201	237	44
Dividend yield (%)	2.4	2.2	2.1	2.2	2.4	2.7	—

5-year stock growth (late-1999 to late-2004): 23 percent ($40 to $49)

Air Products and Chemicals, Inc. 95

7201 Hamilton Blvd.
Allentown, PA 18195
610-481-4911

NYSE: APD
www.airproducts.com

Chairman and CEO: John P. Jones, III

Current Yield	2.3%	
Back-to-the-Future Yield	**5-year** **2.6%**	**10-year** **4.4%**

Rating

Dividend Yield	
Dividend Growth	☆
Consistency	☆ ☆ ☆ ☆
Financial Strength	
Total	**5 points**

IT'S NOT QUITE LIKE CHARGING FOR AIR, BUT AIR PRODUCTS DOES PULL ITS profits from thin air. The Allentown, Pennsylvania operation is a global leader in the sale of gas—as in oxygen, nitrogen, helium, hydrogen, and carbon monoxide—as well as other chemical components used by industrial manufactures and medical equipment makers.

Air Products has operations in more than 30 countries. In addition to the medical supplies industry, the company deals with chemical manufacturers, steel makers, energy companies, food producers, and electronics manufacturers.

Air Products delivers its various vapors via three different modes:

On-site or pipeline. For large industrial users, the company actually builds a plant next to the company's facility or pumps the gas in by pipeline from a nearby supply station.

Liquid bulk. The firm may ship smaller volumes of industrial gas products by tanker trucks or tube trailers.

Packaged gases. Industrial and specialty and medical gases are sometimes delivered in cylinders and bottles.

The company also produces chemical intermediaries used in the production of pesticides, coatings, adhesives and other applications.

Founded in 1940, Air Products has about 110,000 employees and a market capitalization of about $11.5 billion.

Dividend Yield
2.3 percent (2004)

Dividend Growth (past five years)   ☆
38 percent

Consistency   ☆ ☆ ☆ ☆
Increased dividends more than 15 consecutive years.

Financial Strength
Increased earnings per share only one of the past five years.
Increased revenues four of the past five years.

Financial Summary
Fiscal year ended: Dec. 31

	1998	1999	2000	2001	2002	2003	5-Year Growth (%)
Dividends/share ($)	.64	.70	.74	.78	.82	.88	38
Earnings/share ($)	2.22	2.09	2.46	2.36	2.31	2.22	0
Revenue ($billions)	4.92	5.02	5.47	5.72	5.40	6.30	28
Dividend yield (%)	1.6	1.9	2.4	1.9	1.8	2.0	—

5-year stock growth (mid-1999 to mid-2004): 46 percent ($35 to $51)

Dominion Resources, Inc.

P.O. Box 26532
Richmond, VA 23261
804-819-2000

NYSE: D
www.dom.com

Chairman and CEO: Thomas E. Capps
President: Thomas F. Farrell II

Current Yield	4.1%	
Back-to-the-Future Yield	5-year 6.2%	10-year 6.7%

Rating

Dividend Yield	☆ ☆ ☆
Dividend Growth	
Consistency	
Financial Strength	☆
Total	4 points

DOMINION RESOURCES IS THE PARENT COMPANY OF VIRGINIA POWER, WHICH provides electricity and natural gas to more than 2 million customers in Virginia and northeastern North Carolina.

Dominion distributes both electricity and natural gas to its residential and commercial customers. It operates 7,900 miles of natural gas pipeline, and produces more than 24,000 megawatts of electrical power. It has 6.4 trillion cubic feet equivalent of natural gas reserves. The company also has the nation's largest natural gas storage system with more than 960 billion cubic feet of storage capacity.

The Richmond-based operation does most of its business in Virginia, but also provides power for residents in eight other states. In all, it serves more than 5 million customers in nine states.

In addition to its utility services, Dominion has active drilling operations in seven North American basins. Its daily gas and oil production is about 1.2 billion cubic feet equivalent.

Dominion has about 16,700 employees and a market capitalization of about $20 billion.

Dividend Yield ☆ ☆ ☆
4.1 percent (2004)

Dividend Growth (past five years)

Consistency
Increased only once in the past 10 years.

Financial Strength
Increased earnings per share three of the past five years.
Increased revenues three of the past five years.

Summary
Fiscal year ended: Dec. 31

	1998	1999	2000	2001	2002	2003	5-Year Growth(%)
Dividends/share ($)	2.58	2.58	2.58	2.58	2.58	2.58	0
Earnings/share ($)	1.72	2.99	2.50	2.97	4.82	3.91	127
Revenue ($billions)	6.1	5.5	9.3	10.6	10.2	12.1	98
Dividend yield (%)	6.1	5.9	5.3	4.1	4.4	4.3	—

5-year stock growth (mid-1999 to mid-2004): 35 percent ($48 to $65)

Alliance Capital Management, L.P. 97

1345 Avenue of the Americas
New York, NY 10105
212-969-1000

NYSE: AC
www.alliancecapital.com

Chairman and CEO: Bruce W. Calvert

Current Yield	5.1%	
Back-to-the-Future Yield	5-year 4.5%	10-year 11.8%

Rating

Dividend Yield	☆ ☆ ☆ ☆
Dividend Growth	
Consistency	
Financial Strength	
Total	4 points

ALLIANCE CAPITAL IS ONE OF THE NATION'S LEADING INVESTMENT companies. It offers over 100 mutual funds as well as pension management services for many of the world's largest corporations. It also provides investment management services for endowments, banks and insurance companies. In all, Alliance has about $470 billion of assets under management.

After offering one of the best dividends on the market for more than 10 consecutive years, Alliance hit some troubled times during the market downturn, and cut its dividend. But the company has announced plans to return its dividend to previous levels.

The New York operation manages public retirement funds in 35 states. It also has 36 offices in 19 countries.

Alliance Capital markets its line of mutual funds through brokers, financial advisers, banks and insurance agents. Its family of about 120 mutual funds includes a wide range of stock and bond funds, along with about 25 cash management funds, 15 closed-end funds traded on the New York Stock Exchange, a group of funds for foreign investors, and a variety of variable annuity policies.

In all, the company has about 7 million mutual fund clients, and 2,100 institutional clients. The company's leading mutual fund segment is its equity and balanced funds, followed by taxable fixed income funds, tax exempt fixed income funds, and closed-end funds.

Alliance was founded in 1962 as the investment management department of Donaldson, Lufkin & Jenrette to specialize in pension fund management. In 1985 it was acquired by The Equitable Life Assurance Society, which took Alliance public with an initial stock offering in 1988. The Equitable still holds about 57 percent of Alliance stock.

Alliance, which is technically a limited partnership, has about 4,100 employees and a market capitalization of about $13 billion.

Dividend Yield ☆ ☆ ☆ ☆
4.1 percent (2004)

Dividend Growth (past five years)
23 percent

Consistency
The company has cut its dividends each of the past three years, but it has announced plans to return the dividend to previous levels.

Financial Strength
Increased earnings per share only two of the past five years.
Increased revenues only three of the past five years.

Financial Summary
Fiscal year ended: Dec. 31

	1998	1999	2000	2001	2002	2003	5-Year Growth (%)
Dividends/share ($)	1.60	2.49	3.18	2.84	2.30	1.97	23
Earnings/share ($)	1.66	2.53	3.12	2.77	2.19	2.12	28
Revenue ($billions)	1.32	1.87	2.52	3.0	2.74	2.73	107
Dividend yield (%)	6.5	8.8	7.1	5.7	6.2	6.0	—

5-year stock growth (late-1999 to late-2004): 19 percent ($32 to $38)

Verizon Communications, Inc.   98

1095 Avenue of the Americas
New York, NY 10036
212-395-1525

NYSE: VZ
www.verizon.com

Chairman and CEO: Ivan Seidenberg

Current Yield	3.8%	
Back-to-the-Future Yield	5-year 2.5%	10-year 5.7%

Rating

Dividend Yield	☆ ☆
Dividend Growth	
Consistency	
Financial Strength	☆ ☆
Total	**4 points**

FORMED THROUGH THE MERGER OF GTE AND BELL ATLANTIC IN 2000, Verizon is the nation's largest provider of standard phone service and wireless service.

The New York operation also offers communications services in other parts of North America, South America, and Europe.

It is also the world's largest publisher of telephone directories.

In the U.S., Verizon provides phone services in 29 states and Washington, D.C. In all, it has 140 million lines in service in the U.S. Among its services are voice and data transport, enhanced and custom calling features, network access, directory assistance, private lines and public telephones. It also offers long distance services, customer premises equipment distribution, data solutions and systems integration, billing and collections, Internet access services, and inventory management services.

The company has nearly 38 million wireless customers. Verizon offers wireless services in all 50 states and 21 countries.

The company has about 200,000 employees and a market capitalization of about $100 billion.

Dividend Yield   ☆ ☆
3.8 percent (2004)

Dividend Growth (past five years)
None

Consistency
No dividend increases since 1998.

Financial Strength   ☆ ☆
Increased earnings per share three of the past five years.
Increased revenues five of the past five years.

Financial Summary
Fiscal year ended: Dec. 31

	1998	1999	2000	2001	2002	2003	5-Year Growth (%)
Dividends/share ($)	1.54	1.54	1.54	1.54	1.54	1.54	0
Earnings/share ($)	1.79	2.97	4.31	.14	1.49	1.12	—
Revenue ($billions)	57.1	58.2	64.7	67.2	67.6	67.8	19
Dividend yield (%)	2.2	1.8	2.2	2.4	3.5	5.8	—

5-year stock growth (mid-1999 to mid-2004): -41 percent ($68 to $40)

Spain Fund

1345 Avenue of the Americas
New York, NY 10105
800-221-5672

NYSE: SNF

Chairman and President: Dave H. Williams

Current Yield	9.1%	
Back-to-the-Future Yield	5-year 5.8%	10-year 7.2%

Rating

Dividend Yield	☆ ☆ ☆ ☆
Dividend Growth	
Consistency	
Financial Strength	
Total	**4 points**

TECHNICALLY, THIS IS A MUTUAL FUND RATHER THAN A STOCK, BUT WITH A dividend yield of about 9 percent, the Spain Fund should be a tempting choice for anyone interested in income. As a closed-end mutual fund, the Spain Fund trades like a stock on the New York Stock Exchange.

The Spain Fund invests in a wide selection of stocks on the Spanish stock exchange.

Financial services stocks account for about 29 percent of assets, consumer services stocks make up 26 percent, utilities account for 25 percent, energy comprises 8 percent, capital goods stocks make up 4 percent, and technology accounts for 2 percent. About 4 percent of assets are invested in other types of investments.

The Spain Fund has a market capitalization of about $75 million.

Dividend Yield
☆ ☆ ☆ ☆

9.1 percent (2004)

Dividend Growth (past five years)
Dividends have declined

Consistency
Dividends have increased only one of the past five years.

Financial Strength
Increased earnings per share only once in the past five years.

Financial Summary
Fiscal year ended: Dec. 31

	1998	1999	2000	2001	2002	2003	5-Year Growth (%)
Dividends/share ($)	1.50	1.77	1.46	1.01	.76	.63	—
Earnings/share ($)	.04	-0.7	-.13	-.03	-.03	.01	—
Assets ($millions)	205	141	89	73	59	74	—
Dividend yield (%)	10.7	12.3	12.3	11.7	11.9	8.3	—

5-year stock growth (mid-1999 to mid-2004): -33 percent ($15 to $10)

Marathon Oil Corp.

100

5555 San Felipe Road
Houston, TX 77056
713-629-6600

NYSE: MRO
www.marathon.com

Chairman: Thomas Usher
CEO and president: Clarence Cazelot, Jr.

Current Yield	3.0%	
Back-to-the-Future Yield	5-year 3.8%	10-year 5.5%

Rating

Dividend Yield	☆ ☆
Dividend Growth	
Consistency	
Financial Strength	☆ ☆
Total	4 points

MARATHON OIL IS THE NATION'S FOURTH LARGEST OIL AND GAS COMPANY and the fifth largest refiner and marketer of oil products. Founded in 1877, Marathon is involved in virtually every phase of the oil production process, including exploration, development, production, refining, transportation, and marketing.

The Houston-based operation conducts its exploration activities primarily in the U.S., the United Kingdom, Angola, Canada, and Norway. The firm also has production operations in several countries, including Russia. It recently acquired a Russian production company, Khanty Mansiysk Oil Corp.

The company produces crude oil and natural gas in seven countries, with daily production of about 194,000 barrels of oil and 1,147 million cubic feet of gas.

Marathon sells gasoline through 5,700 outlets, including its namesake Marathon stations, as well as stations operated by its subsidiaries under the names Speedway and SuperAmerica. Through a joint venture with Pilot Corp., the company also operates 270 travel centers.

Marathon explores for oil on land and sea. Much of its exploration efforts are focused on deepsea areas outside of Angola, Eastern Canada and the Gulf of Mexico. Its production facilities are concentrated in four key areas, North America, Europe, Africa, and Russia.

The company has about 28,000 employees and a market capitalization of about $12 billion.

Dividend Yield ☆ ☆
3.0 percent (2004)

Dividend Growth (past five years)
14 percent

Consistency
Increased dividends only six of the past 10 years.

Financial Strength ☆ ☆
Increased earnings per share four of the past five years.
Increased revenue three of the past five years.

Financial Summary
Fiscal year ended: Dec. 31

	1998	1999	2000	2001	2002	2003	5-Year Growth (%)
Dividends/share ($)	.84	.84	.88	.92	.92	.96	14
Earnings/share ($)	1.09	1.40	4.20	4.26	1.81	3.26	199
Revenue ($billions)	71.6	78.0	96.9	91.6	88.7	118.2	65
Dividend yield (%)	2.5	3.0	3.4	3.2	3.6	3.7	—

5-year stock growth (late-1999 to late-2004): 19 percent ($29 to $37)

The 100 Best by Location

Alabama
AmSouth Bancorp
Regions Financial Corp.

Arizona
Pinnacle West Capital Corp.

Arkansas
Alltel Corp.

California
ABM Industries
Avery Dennison
California Water Service Group
ChevronTexaco Corp.
Health Care Property Investors, Inc.
Mercury General Corp.
Wells Fargo & Co.

Colorado
Archstone-Smith Trust

Connecticut
General Electric Company
Peoples Bank
Pitney Bowes, Inc.
Stanley Works

Delaware
MBNA Corp.
Wilmington Trust Corp.

Florida
FPL Group, Inc.

Georgia
BellSouth Corp.
Coca-Cola Company
Genuine Parts Company
SunTrust Banks
Synovus Financial

Illinois
Abbott Laboratories
Equity Residential Properties Trust
Peoples Energy Corp.
R. R. Donnelley & Sons Company
Sara Lee Corp.
ServiceMaster Corp.
Unitrin, Inc.

Indiana
Duke Realty Corp.

Iowa
Bandag, Inc.

Louisiana
Entergy Corp.

Massachusetts
NSTAR

Michigan
Comerica, Inc.

Minnesota
TCF Financial
U.S. Bancorp

Missouri
Ameren Corp.
Emerson Electric Company
Great Plains Energy, Inc.
May Department Stores

Nebraska
ConAgra Foods, Inc.

New Jersey
Johnson & Johnson
Mack-Cali Realty Corp.
Merck & Company
New Jersey Resources Corp.

New Mexico
Thornburg Mortgage

New York
Alliance Capital Management, L.P.
Astoria Financial Corp.
Bristol-Myers Squibb Company
Consolidated Edison, Inc.
Energy East Corp.
Kimco Realty Corp.
National Fuel Gas Co.
New Plan Excel Realty Trust
North Fork Bancorp
Spain Fund
Verizon Communications

North Carolina
BB&T Corp.
Bank of America
Jefferson-Pilot Corp.
Piedmont Natural Gas Co.
Progress Energy
VF Corp.

Ohio
Cedar Fair, L.P.
Cincinnati Financial Corp.
Cinergy Corp.
Fifth Third Bancorp
Procter & Gamble Company
RPM International, Inc.

Pennsylvania
Air Products and Chemicals, Inc.
Buckeye Partners, L.P.
Liberty Property Trust
Lincoln National Corp.
PPG Industries, Inc.
Quaker Chemical Corp.

South Dakota
Black Hills Corp.

Tennessee
First Horizon National
Healthcare Realty Trust

Texas
Atmos Energy Corp.
Exxon Mobil Corp.
Kimberly-Clark Corp.
Kinder Morgan Energy Partners
Marathon Oil Corp.
SBC Communications, Inc.
Teppco Partners, L.P.
Weingarten Realty Investors

Virginia
Dominion Resources, Inc.

Washington
Washington Federal, Inc.

Wisconsin
Associated Banc-Corp.
WPS Resources Corp.

Canada
Bank of Nova Scotia
Canadian Imperial Bank of Commerce
National Bank of Canada
Royal Bank of Canada
TransCanada Corp.

France
Total S.A.

Mexico
Telefonos de Mexico S.A.

New Zealand
Telecom Corp. of New Zealand (ADS)

The 100 Best by Industry

Apparel
V.F. Corp.

Banks
AmSouth Bancorp
Associated Banc-Corp.
Astoria Financial Corp.
Bank of America
Bank of Nova Scotia
BB&T Corp.
Canadian Imperial Bank of Commerce
Comerica, Inc.
Fifth Third Bancorp
First Horizon National
National Bank of Canada
North Fork Bancorp
Peoples Bank
Regions Financial Corp.
Royal Bank of Canada
SunTrust Banks
Synovus Financial
TCF Financial
U.S. Bancorp
Washington Federal, Inc.
Wells Fargo & Co.
Wilmington Trust Corp.

Chemicals and coatings
Air Products and Chemicals, Inc.
Quaker Chemical Corp.
PPG Industries, Inc.
RPM International, Inc.

Consumer and commercial products
Avery Dennison
Bandag, Inc.
Genuine Parts Company
Kimberly-Clark Corp.
Procter & Gamble Company
Stanley Works

Consumer and commercial services
ABM Industries
R. R. Donnelley & Sons Co.
ServiceMaster Company

Energy
Buckeye Partners, L.P.
ChevronTexaco Corp.
Exxon Mobil Corp.
Kimco Realty Corp.
Kinder Morgan Energy Partners
Marathon Oil Corp.
Teppco Partners, L.P.
Total S.A.
TransCanada Corp.

Financial
Alliance Capital Management
MBNA Corp.
Spain Fund

Foods
Coca-Cola Company
ConAgra Foods, Inc.
Sara Lee Corp.

Health care and medical
Abbott Laboratories
Bristol-Myers Squibb
Johnson & Johnson
Merck & Company

Household and commercial furnishings
Emerson Electric Company
General Electric Company

Insurance

Cincinnati Financial Corp.
Jefferson-Pilot Corp.
Lincoln National Corp.
Mercury General Corp.
Unitrin, Inc.

Office and computer equipment

Pitney Bowes, Inc.

Real Estate Investment Trusts (REITs)

Archstone-Smith Trust
Duke Realty Corp.
Equity Residential Properties Trust
Health Care Property Investors, Inc.
Healthcare Realty Trust
Liberty Property Trust
Mack-Cali Realty Corp.
New Plan Excel Realty Trust
Thornburg Mortgage
Weingarten Realty Investors

Recreation

Cedar Fair, L.P.

Retail

May Department Stores

Telecommunications

Alltel Corp.
BellSouth Corp.
SBC Communications, Inc.
Telecom Corp. of New Zealand
Telefonos de Mexico S.A.
Verizon Communications, Inc.

Utilities

Ameren Corp.
Atmos Energy Corp.
Black Hills Corp.
California Water Service Group
Cinergy Corp.
Consolidated Edison, Inc.
Dominion Resources, Inc.
Energy East Corp.
Entergy Corp.
FPL Group
Great Plains Energy, Inc.
National Fuel Gas Co.
New Jersey Resources Corp.
NSTAR
Peoples Energy Corp.
Piedmont Natural Gas Co.
Pinnacle West Capital Corp.
Progress Energy
WPS Resources Corp.

Index

AUDIOCASSETTES

How To Get Rich and Stay Rich
A Live Speech by Fred J. Young   **Retail Price: $5.95**

This popular and humorous speech by Fred J. Young explains how this multimillionaire made his fortune by investing a portion of his salary in a few shares of stock on a regular basis. At this time, his net worth is over $3 million.

Don't Get Mad — Get Rich
A Live Speech by Fred J. Young   **Retail Price: $5.95**

Humorous true adventures that Fred J. Young had during his journey toward becoming a multimillionaire. Fun to listen to and full of stock market wisdom.

BOOKS

The 100 Best Dividend-Paying Stocks To Own In America
Updated yearly
Author: Gene Walden   **Retail Price: $19.95**

Making Dollars With Pennies:
How the Small Investor Can Beat the Wizards on Wall Street
Author: R. Max Bowser   **Retail Price: $19.95**

Penny Stock Winners:
True Stories of Successful Investors
Author: R. Max Bowser   **Retail Price: $19.95**

Guaranteed Profits With Small Stocks:
The Only Stock Market Investment System
That Comes With A $5,000 Guarantee
Author: R. Max Bowser   **Retail Price: $19.95**